That One Girl

Lessons from Mary for young Catholic Women

◯ LIFE TEEN

Published by Life Teen, Inc.
2222 S. Dobson Rd.
Suite 601
Mesa, AZ 85202
LifeTeen.com

Printed in the United States of America.
Printed on acid-free paper.

For more information about Life Teen or to order additional copies, go online to LifeTeen.com or call us at 1-800-809-3902.

This book is
dedicated to all the
girls who, like me, are
trying so hard to figure
out what it means to be an
authentic, Catholic woman.
And to Mary, that one girl
who figured it out... thanks
for always being there
for me. You're the best
mama a girl could
ask for.

Table of Contents

Introduction

If you're reading this, there are two things you need to know. The first thing is that I've been praying for you. Yes, you.

I didn't need to know your name, or where you live. If you're holding this book, that means you have a soul (unless this book survived the apocalypse and you're a zombie). And because you have a soul, I already feel close to you. I'm your sister because we have the same heavenly Father. God created us both and the only way to get through this crazy thing called life is to help each other out.

So I've been praying for you. I prayed that you would know that I genuinely care about you. I want you to understand how much you are loved, how much you have to offer to the world, and how much our mother Mary wants to walk with you throughout your life. She cares about you personally.

Secondly, I need to get this out right away… I'm not perfect. I'm here to tell you that our Blessed Mother is the most amazing woman I've ever encountered. I'm here to tell you that throughout my life, she has taught me some of the most important lessons I know. But I'm also here to tell you, I'm not done learning and I'm just as human as you are.

I have dry hair and I think my feet are too big. Some days, when everything aligns just right and I'm convinced the world is out to get me, I have to scream in a pillow and I need a freshly baked chocolate chip cookie.

I've made mistakes, just like you, and I've shed a lot of tears over my mistakes. Some were really big and I'm still dealing with the consequences. Some just felt really big but were actually pretty small and were forgotten in a couple days.

This book is about some of the things that I've struggled with the most and what I've learned through Mary's example. I'm not going to assume that you struggle with the same things I struggle with. We're all beautifully different. But I bet you'll be able to relate to my story, because I know these are issues that a lot of girls have encountered. Living in a girl's dorm for four years in college was essentially a constant chorus of "that happens to you too?" "you feel like that too?" "isn't that the worst?"

My hope is that my witness of shortcomings, failures, and lessons learned the hard way will help you along your path to holiness too.

I was watching TV the other day and heard a girl describe a mother as "the girl that goes before you in the world and shows you how to do stuff." That's who Mary is for you and I. She went before us and experienced everything a normal girl does (minus texting and sin) and left us an example to follow. She showed us how to be a girl —what true femininity means, how to handle emotions, and what it means to trust even if you've been hurt.

She was just an ordinary girl. She wasn't a celebrity of her day. She was human... normal. She was just "that one girl." But she became that one girl that changed the course of history.

You and I, in the grand scheme of things, are very small people. In my family, at my school, in my country, and in my world — I'm just one girl. What can one girl do?

She can become a saint, leave a legacy, and impact the culture... just by being the best girl she can be.

That's what I'm striving for and that's my hope for you too. It's my prayer that this book helps you along the way and if it does... don't thank me — thank God that He gave us His mother Mary as a model for us.

I'm praying for you.

Perfectionism:
The Steps to Perfection

Hi, my name is Christina, and I suffer from a case of approval addiction. I love having the approval of everyone around me. Scratch that, I *need* the approval of everyone around me. This hasn't worked out so well for me considering that I haven't figured out how to be *perfect* yet.

One of the things I haven't mastered is the beautiful and graceful Belle-in-a-ball-gown staircase descent. I'm more like the beast... but with a sprained ankle, trying not to spill my coffee. I've accepted this fact though — stairs and I don't get along. I'm talented on violin. I can draw a beautiful portrait. I make brownies to die for. But stairs? One of the most basic human activities besides getting a spoon to your mouth... I am challenged by.

Don't judge me though for not being able to walk while ascending or descending with a 100 percent success rate; it's not my fault, stairs are out to get me.

I don't know about you, but I was super awkward as a pre-teen. Sometimes I actually get jealous when I see 11-year-olds who have fashion sense. When I was that age I was all awkward and self-conscious and had no idea that becoming an awesome woman like the cousin I idealized came with so many weird body things and a storm of emotions.

Some days I'm pretty sure that only my fashion sense has graduated and moved on from that awkward stage. At least that's how I feel when I do something that is totally humiliating. You know when you just want to press "undo" on your last sentence, joke, outburst, or clumsy movement?

"The peak of perfection lies in our wanting to be what God wants us to be."

-St. Jane de Chantal

It's like being 11 again. That was the first time a staircase dramatically attacked me. My dad, two of my sisters, and I were going to church to see a Christian concert. As we were walking up the steps I tripped (because gosh that's just what happens when you're 11, okay?).

As I was falling I heard one of the most awful sounds in the world: ripping fabric. I felt a pit in my stomach and my embarrassment went right to my cheeks. I looked down in horror at my dress which now had a rip about six inches long on my right hip. This would have been hard to tell my mom, but telling my dad was even worse! I have no memory of how we talked about it except that my dad said it would be fine and we were not going to go home.

I was not fine. I was mortified. I was ashamed of tripping. I was terrified that someone would notice that I was clutching the side of my dress closed to avoid everyone seeing my underwear. I hated that I had fallen on the stairs, and I counted down the minutes until we could go home.

At one point, the singer even invited all the kids to stand and sing with her. And guess who went up? Everyone but *me*. Because I thought was *stupid*. And clumsy. And the perfection I wanted seemed so far out of reach. I had such a high and unrealistic expectation for my every word and action. My version of "perfect" was all about achievements, appearances, and proper performance. Sure, it included virtue because I also wanted to be a good, holy person... but being virtuous wasn't the only thing I cared about. It wasn't even on the top of the list. (I think "be as cool as a Disney Channel star" occupied that top spot.)

Now, of course God calls each of us to strive for perfect virtue. Jesus encourages us to "be perfect as your heavenly Father is perfect" (Matthew 5:48). However, to imitate that perfect love and mercy of God is something that takes a lifetime to achieve. That kind of perfect has nothing to do with always having your nails nicely manicured — something that was included in my definition of perfect.

It's impossible to live up to the expectations I had for myself and trying so hard only made me unhappy. I couldn't shake this negative attitude about myself as I grew up and it trailed me as closely as my shadow.

My nemesis, the stairs, didn't help. When I was a teen, my family lived in a house with carpeted stairs. Carpet on stairs is the equivalent to sharp teeth on an already menacing creature. One day as I was minding my own business, just trying to get downstairs, I felt that rare but terrible sinking feeling in my stomach — that feeling that means buckle up, watch out, disaster is about to strike. I knew what was going to happen before it did. My feet were moving too fast; I wasn't being careful.

My foot slipped off the step and my hope for a successful descent was doomed. I went crashing down the remaining stairs and while no, my life did not flash before my eyes, I did have one last, deep, and profound thought... "ahhhhhhhhhhh!"

Lying in a heap on the floor, I couldn't tell which hurt more — my back, my shoulder, my foot, or my dignity. At least this incident would get me some good attention. You see, being the fifth of six children meant I would not only go to great lengths for attention, but also saw every mishap as a lucky break in my constant search for sympathy.

"What were you *doing*? Why weren't you more *careful*?"

The sound of my dad's irritated voice snapped me out of my dreams of a sympathetic family group hug around Christina.

Tears came to my eyes. All I wanted was to be perfect but I had both the Mead genes (which included "hopelessly clumsy") and Mead jeans (the fifth child hand-me-downs-you'll-never-be-fashionable brand).

Instances like this one further ingrained in me the reality of my imperfection. When faced with failure, even something small like falling down (or *up*, let's be real, that's a thing too) the stairs, I became all the more resolute to strive to become perfect.

I was annoyed with myself. I was annoyed with staircases. And, can I be honest with you? I was pretty annoyed with the Blessed Mother too.

I was annoyed with Mary, the Mother of God, because she is *immaculate*. She was born without Original Sin. That means she is *perfect* then, right? It seems like Mary is everything I wanted but that I couldn't be. So how could I love having her as my role model? Have you ever thought about that? It can make Mary seem so totally unrelatable, right?

This was a huge hurdle I had to get over. In college I took a whole class about Mary and throughout the class, every time my male professor gushed (is there a male version of the word "gushed"?) about how wonderful Mary is and what a great role model she is, and how she was such a great mother (and so on for 75 minutes twice a week), all I could think was "but everything was so *easy* for her because she was *perfect*."

My professor didn't know what it was like to be a woman. He didn't understand the struggles, temptations, and pressures we face as women. How could *he* know what kind of role model we needed? I was more comfortable looking up to someone like St. Teresa of Avila as my role model. She struggled a lot with sin and her prayer life, and I could relate more to that than someone who was perfect. I felt guilty for not loving Mary like everyone else, but I couldn't find a way to get over my frustration with her for being so perfect.

It's hard to love someone who has something that you desire but feel like you can never attain in this life.

I can never be perfect, according to what my definition of perfection was. This desire to be perfect that I struggle with is called "perfectionism." I would define it as the belief that in order to be loved and accepted (by others and by yourself), you have to be flawless.

This seems to make sense because, after all, if I was perfect I would have more friends. I would get more A's and less B's on my homework. I would be dating right now. I would be the size of that model on the magazine. I wouldn't drop things. I wouldn't trip. I would never disappoint my parents. I would be motivated, patient, and bold. I would, essentially, be superhuman.

Only a superhuman could possibly be like that, and the last time I checked, they only exist in comic books and movies.

I think that this need to be perfect in everything has come from living in a society that says as a woman, you have two options in life in order to prove your worth and make your life valuable. Your options are to seduce or produce.

The world says you should be looking in the mirror and standing on the scale and pinching at any fat you find, taking mental notes of what to work on at the gym. You should spend hundreds of dollars on the newest fashion trends... every season. Please feel free to eat both those pieces of pizza as long as you don't mind the crushing shame and cloud of guilt hanging over you for a week. Don't forget that you're expected to spend half of your life at the gym trying to look like the olympic athlete from the Nike billboard that screams at you "how dare you have a muffin top you gross, flabby, slob of a being" every time you drive by it. We live in a world where people discuss the necessity and attractiveness of a thigh gap. A thigh gap.

Not a compassionate heart. A thigh gap. Why? Because they'd like you to believe that you, my dear, were put in this world only to look pretty and be the kind of girl that turns heads on the street. (And you better just start with the anti-aging cream right now. It's never too soon.)

Unless of course you're going to be the top executive somewhere and be so productive that honey bees want to learn your ways. In that case, it's okay to wear flats and not get the boob job because you *are* busy making six figures and heralding gender equality in the work place. You're showing the world you can work just as hard as a man. Hooray for you. Your life has worth.

"How happy I am to see myself imperfect and be in need of God's Mercy."
-St. Thérèse of Lisieux

And if you don't fit into the seduce or produce boxes... maybe you should just give up, and the "maybe" was generous. Why don't you get off the grid and bake cakes and have babies and grow radishes. If you can't seduce or produce, what does your life even mean?

Alright, I know I got a little carried away and exaggerated.

Actually, no I didn't. This is *literally* what's expected of women by the world. Either be *hot* or prove how *useful* you are to the world. There's no in-between.

Except that there is an in-between and that's where the majority of the population exists. (Except for Beyoncé.)

The truth is that humans fail. We're imperfect and flawed and that's what makes us unique. Guess what? According to the world's standard of "perfect," Mary wasn't perfect either. She was *sinless*. Big difference.

In order to come into this world as an infant, Christ couldn't dwell for nine months inside a body that was tainted by sin. Since God is God, He can do whatever He wants. Mary was able to be sinless because God applied the saving graces of Jesus' death to her. Even though in time, His death happened after Mary's birth, God is outside of time so days and years on a calendar don't restrict Him.

Mary's Immaculate Conception (the phrase that means she was born without the stain of Original Sin) means that she was worthy of being the Mother of God; it also means that she was Satan's worst enemy, and the nicest kid to ever live on the block (did they have "blocks" in Nazareth?).

She never sinned or separated herself from God in any way. But she did have struggles. She tripped and fell too. She probably said the wrong thing sometimes. She was embarrassed. She had temptations.

Just because she never actually committed a sin, like gossip, pride, or disrespecting her parents, doesn't mean that she was free from the situations that would cause her to sin in those ways. It was that her love of God was stronger than her desire to disobey His commandments and hurt Him and the people around her.

I think Mary would be embarrassed if she knew that I was intimidated by her seemingly perfect life. Her sinless nature doesn't make her a worse role model but a better one. When you're looking to be really good at some skill, you don't ask the advice of someone who's only mediocre at that skill. That would be like asking an Olympic athlete to teach you how to knit a sweater.

Maybe there's a cross-country skier who has adopted the hobby of knitting... but let's be real, they're probably pretty busy skiing.

The "skill" we're aiming towards is sainthood — virtue — not flawless stair-mastery. Mary knows how to care about her appearance but not take it to the level of vanity. I'd love to learn that. She knows how to love other people while simultaneously not liking them because of a personality clash. That's something that would be awesome for me to learn. Every person has a unique personality and it's absurd to think that everyone will get along with everyone else; that's impossible in this life... especially since Mary lived among sinners. Mary had a personality; she had certain character traits that may have clashed with someone else. For example, maybe she loved to plan things out, but someone else wasn't a planner... that can be a bit frustrating for both people. We're not expected to get along with and like everyone. I think Mary is no exception to that. Love supercedes "liking" someone because love is a choice, not a feeling. Mary was good at choosing to practice the virtue of charity. That doesn't mean she was "miss perfect" and had crowds of friends.

I can't get annoyed with that Mary.

If sainthood is the goal of our lives, then falling down (or up) the stairs is so *minor*. It's a pride problem. Instead of my faults being another reason to be frustrated, imperfections can be another stepping stone to sainthood.

It's one of my daily struggles - this tension between beating myself up for not being perfect, and letting go and surrendering to the fact that I am not and never will be *perfectly* graceful, tactful, or accomplished.

Recently, I was driving out of the mall parking lot and made a mistake about which lane I needed to be in. I immediately tried to correct my mistake by sharply turning the wheel and inching into the other lane between cars. This resulted in me taking up not *one* but *two* lanes.

The bus driver next to me was soooooo understanding though. NOT. He cursed at me and honked at me as if I was on a mission to get in his way and ruin his day.

I could have felt ashamed for taking the wrong lane and causing that traffic jam. It was a mistake though. And in that moment I looked at the bus driver, shrugged my shoulders, and made a sorry-but-I'm-not-sorry face. Then I went on with my mall exiting and my day.

I shocked even myself. I moved on. I let it go. (These are things I'm not used to doing.) This small victory was cause for a big celebration in my mind. I once had a friend who would always remind me to not get mad at her when she did something that was an accident. Likewise, when she wasn't mad at me for something stupid I did or forgot to do, she reminded me, "I can't get mad over accidents."

That's how you overcome this struggle. The secret is in allowing yourself to simultaneously be flawed and be loved. You have to realize that when people see your faults, they don't recoil in horror and stop loving you. Instead, when others see your faults and imperfections, they only see someone who's like them. No one is perfect. We sometimes fail. We all get a turn to act like an idiot.

This is how you and I overcome the "seduce or produce" culture too. Our worth isn't in being perfect at school, jobs, relationships, or muscle tone. You have worth because you are God's daughter. He made you with a purpose, and He has a plan for your life (Jeremiah 29:11). He made you not because He had to but because He wanted to. His love isn't contingent on your perfection.

The beauty of being Catholic is that we have a whole Church full of really imperfect people. The Bible has so many stories of people that God used to carry out His plan that were big sinners. He used people who had a knack for messing up everything. I haven't met any of them *personally*, but I'm pretty sure that they weren't all the perfect dress size, either.

Perfectionism is a form of spiritual attack because Satan doesn't want you to feel good about yourself. He doesn't want you to walk with confidence in God's mercy. The Blessed Mother is the ideal person to help us in this because she's the best warrior against spiritual attack. She was inaccessible to Satan. She didn't ever give in to his temptations and tactics, and that infuriated him. Also, she was the one that brought God into this world to save a fallen and sinful race — another reason why Satan despises her. In other words, you want Mary on your side to help arm yourself against the enemy. St. Maximilian Kolbe affirmed this when he said,

"The Immaculate alone has from God the promise of victory over Satan. She seeks souls that will consecrate themselves entirely to her, that will become in her hands forceful instruments for the defeat of Satan and the spread of God's Kingdom."

She is the only one whom Satan couldn't get to. Do you know how much that ticked him off? And do you know how much YOU can annoy him by throwing yourself into Mary's arms by seeking refuge in her presence in prayer? She can help you so much in your daily life.

Life doesn't have to be a pursuit of what the world thinks is perfect, just a pursuit of heaven through a lot of imperfect ways — that's what God works through.

"I need nothing but God and to lose myself in the heart of Jesus."

-St. Margaret Mary Alacoque

The next time you want to feel bad about yourself, let God's love for you be stronger than the pressure to be perfect. Say to yourself, "I'm a person who sometimes fails," and give yourself permission to work towards virtue.
I've spent so much of my life worried about what other people think of me, and longing for their approval instead of focusing on what God thinks of me and seeking His approval. I don't want to continue to be that way and Mary's helping me get there.

I'm a person who sometimes trips on stairs. I'm a person who sometimes says the wrong thing. I'm a person who sins. I'm a person who is stumbling and tripping along the road to heaven. I'm a person who sometimes fails.

But Mary is my role model because she was really good at being a saint. She had perfect virtue. Her top priority was to be who God wanted her to be, not who the world expected her to be. That's what I want. How about you?

Body Image:
Does This Look Okay?

Speaking of being perfect, how many times have you wondered if you look good today? I think I'm on number 238.

I'm convinced there are two kinds of people in this world: those who struggle with body image and those who lie about it. I'm not about to lie to you so I'll be vulnerable and tell you that this is something I struggle with.

I can still think back to the time when being self-conscious never even crossed my mind. I wish I could go back there. I never cared what I was wearing, or that my hair was always in a ponytail. I was clueless and innocent and blissfully happy just being me — building forts in the woods and riding my bike.

Then, there was this time when my sisters started talking about how much they weighed, and I became convinced that this was something girls are supposed to care about. Then my physician asked me how I felt about my height and weight compared to my friends. This forced me to compare myself to my friends, something I hadn't thought of before. I began to slowly notice the comments about certain girls being "hot" and I instantly compared what they had and didn't have to myself, taking notes for my mental manual of "what's expected of me."

If you don't struggle with body image right now, chances are you either have struggled with it at some point, you've avoided the sight of every magazine, or you were miraculously blessed with a mother figure so aware of the threats of culture that she proactively taught you the proper attitude about your body.

As girls, we learn a lot from our mothers. If a mom models constant anxiety over her weight, that's what her daughter learns. If a mother models the attitude that the body is something to be hidden and is shameful, that's what a daughter will learn. If a mother models that daily exercise is a fun, fulfilling lifestyle, that's what a daughter will learn. If a mother models high-waisted jeans... actually, you still don't have to wear high-waisted jeans.

The only way to learn something is to have someone else teach you. No 5-year-old wakes up one day doing algebra and hoping to weigh 105 pounds as a college student. Everything is taught to us, either blatantly or subtly through the TV shows we watch, the magazines we read, or someone else's example. When I was 10 years old, my neighbor told me she wanted to be a stripper when she grew up because that's what her sister was; that's the example she had in her life to learn from.

The strongest influence in our lives comes from the people who raise us. From the time we're babies we rely on them and trust them to provide us with our most basic necessities — to keep us safe, fed, and loved. They are *everything* to us and they seem trustworthy and invincible. The things that they teach us, the words they say, the attitudes they exhibit all stay with us until we choose to actively pursue to learn something different.

Most girls don't do that though. They go through life chasing after another form of perfection — the perfect appearance. Which, as I mentioned before, is because we live in this "seduce or produce" culture, and the seduce part is more immediately gratifying.

Sometimes I think every single one of us has an unhealthy view on food. So few people have a healthy attitude about food and exercise. Instead, it's feelings of guilt about eating butter on your bagel, guilt over eating the cinnamon bagel instead of the multi-grain one, or even over eating a bagel at all when a black coffee would have been fewer calories.

Life becomes about punishing yourself for any bad food choices. And then, when you make healthy, low calorie choices, you reward yourself with a chocolate milkshake, which is then a bad choice and must be punished. It's an endless and miserable cycle. If it's not shame over calories, it's an attitude that food is one thing you can control in your life, rather than the one thing you need to stay healthy.

I've been on both ends of the spectrum and I'm not proud of the unhealthy attitudes about food I had. I wish I could take it back, but no one taught me otherwise. There have been times I've gone to bed hungry because I felt I had made a "bad" food choice earlier in the day. There were also times in high school when I sat on the floor of my closet sobbing after refusing to eat dinner as an act of rebellion against my parents.

Your body and the food God has blessed us with are very, very good things. It's the good things that are the most attacked by Satan. He tries to make you believe you'll never be pretty enough, or thin enough, and that you have to be perfectly beautiful in order for others to truly love you.

Where do you stop when your goal is to be "perfectly beautiful"? It's never enough to get to a certain size. The number on the scale has the potential to always look too large and shameful. It has become normal to hate your body. And I'm tired of it.

I'm tired of seeing men give more attention to their waitresses than their wives. I'm tired of hearing guys say they'll only go somewhere if hot girls will be there. I'm tired of beautiful girls calling themselves fat, tearing themselves down because confidence doesn't feel right. I'm tired of the pressure to look a certain way in order to please a guy.

There was one time I was surfing the Internet while sitting next to a guy I had a crush on. I started looking at a shoe store online and my crush began giving me his opinion on all the different kinds of shoes that girls wear and what he likes, doesn't like, what he thinks is hot and what's totally not.

I laughed it off, and probably made some stupid comment about not caring what he thought. But let's be real, when you have a crush on someone you hang on their every word and replay every conversation in your head.

I always said I wouldn't ever change who I was for a guy. I didn't want to be that girl whose world revolved around pleasing whomever her new crush was. And yet, for a couple months, I became that girl. I couldn't believe that while I was shopping for shoes I was comparing them to the standard of what my crush would like, not what *my* personal preference was.

I just wanted to feel confident. My definition of confident was whatever this one guy would like to see me wear. Isn't confidence what the struggle with self-esteem is all about? It's a constant search for the confidence that was stolen from us when we were little girls. Someone, somewhere convinced us that we are not enough. We believed the lie. And that lie has held us captive.

The enemy loves to keep us stuck on that lie. He has managed, through the influence of our culture, to convince us that our bodies are the most important thing about us. Blessed Pope John Paul II lamented this when he said:

> *"Yet how many women have been and continue to be valued more for their physical appearance than for their skill, their professionalism, their intellectual abilities, their deep sensitivity; in a word, the very dignity of their being!" (Letter of Pope John Paul II to Women)*

The world is *always* going to push this standard on us. We have to be the ones to rebel. We can be a generation of girls who say, "No, I am more than my body." Before we can be anything, we must believe we are more than our bodies. This is the real challenge, especially when we've been deprived of anyone who would teach us this truth.

I want affirmation, and at times, I crave a guy's attention because it says, "You're worth it, you're precious to me, you're enough." Those are the words my mind often waits to hear, so I look for someone to tell me because I don't ever tell myself. The most obvious way I know how to get that affirmation and attention is by using my body. I'm not alone. Look around at the fashion trends. More skin equals sexier and sexier equals attention. Are the clothes on the racks designed to reveal our inner beauty (soul) or only draw attention to our outer beauty (body)?

If I'm always in search of a more perfect body and style, that seems like a sure way of getting attention and being assured of my worth. I wish I had known sooner what a recipe for disaster this is.

It leaves girls leaning over the toilet and living on the treadmill. And at the next family party when the first thing everyone says is "You look great! Have you lost weight?" you know you're doing something right because the goal always was, first and foremost, to look *great*.

This obsession over our appearance can actually become like a false idol — something you've placed in the number one spot in your life instead of God. When God is first in your life, He brings peace, happiness, and joy. Idolizing the perfect body image is a very self-centered pursuit. It does give us a very temporary sense of satisfaction and fulfillment, but once that ends, you're only left feeling unhappy again.

Because it's *shallow*! Like "don't dive in or you'll break your neck" shallow! I'm not trying to minimize the fact that this is a real struggle; however, I think if we refocus on what's truly important we can regain confidence in how God made each of us unique and we'll be motivated to pursue a healthy lifestyle instead of the ups and downs of dieting and binging.

> "Christ made my soul beautiful with the jewels of grace and virtue. I belong to Him who the angels serve."
>
> —St. Agnes

The first step is realizing what a beautiful creation the female body is.

What if teenaged Mary sometimes felt inadequate too? She had saintly parents: St. Anne and St. Joachim. She didn't grow up with the same media messages (or any actually — I'm positive TV and MTV didn't exist) as we have. She lived her life totally committed to God and virtue. However, she wasn't immune from the competition among her friends. Sarah could weave the best basket, Beth could bake everyone's favorite bread, and Hannah made the top selling garments, but what was Mary known for? She wasn't sheltered from the sinful, prideful, and petty nature of her girlfriends. Did she ever feel like she didn't measure up? Did she feel a little self-conscious that her hair wasn't as long and luscious as the other girls? Did she have fleeting moments of worry that she wasn't good enough?

I can't tell you if she was the best at anything *besides* being humble and offering everything to God. Her sinless nature meant she didn't give in to jealousy or vanity, or distrust in God's plan for her, but I have to wonder, did her prayer ever sound like this?

"God, I know you knit me in my mother's womb exactly how you intended me to be. Help me to believe that more and more every day."

When Mary was a young teenager, an angel from God named Gabriel appeared to her and let her know what God's grand design was for her life, if she wanted to participate in it.

Take a look, I've added some ideas about what a young teenager like Mary *might* have been thinking:

> *And coming to her, he said, "Hail, favored one! The Lord is with you." But she was greatly troubled at what was said and pondered what sort of greeting this might be (**Luke 1:28-29**).*

("Favored one? I'm just a simple girl. It's Hannah who everyone loves the most. I'm confused and afraid... ")

> *Then the angel said to her, "Do not be afraid, Mary, for you have found favor with God. Behold, you will conceive in your womb and bear a son, and you shall name him Jesus. He will be great and will be called Son of the Most High, and the Lord God will give him the throne of David his father, and he will rule over the house of Jacob forever, and of his kingdom there will be no end" (**Luke 1:30-33**).*

("I know what that all means. I've read those prophecies in Scripture so often. But God knows I've vowed to remain a virgin...")

> *But Mary said to the angel, "How can this be, since I have no relations with a man?"*

> *And the angel said to her in reply, "The holy Spirit will come upon you, and the power of the Most High will overshadow you. Therefore the child to be born will be called holy, the Son of God (**Luke 1:34-35**).*

("Oh, well that explains that.")

> *And behold, Elizabeth, your relative, has also conceived a son in her old age, and this is the sixth month for her who was called barren; for nothing will be impossible for God." Mary said,*

"Behold, I am the handmaid of the Lord. May it be done to me according to your word."

*Then the angel departed from her (**Luke 1:36-38**).*

("So... That escalated quickly and now my life is totally different... How am I going to tell my parents?! How am I supposed to tell Joseph?!")

This moment is known as the Incarnation – when God became an itty-bitty baby in Mary's womb. She became the spouse of the Holy Spirit and accepted a role in the salvation of mankind. If she ever felt inadequate, here was the antidote. God called her His "favored one" (Luke 1:28). Talk about affirmation. He also chose her to give the second person of the Trinity, the Son of God, a human body.

She literally carried God in her body. There's no other way to say that. Well, actually, there's a one-word way of saying it. It's a theological name that's been given to Mary as one of her titles: "**Theotokos**" from the Greek word "Theo" meaning "God," and "tokos" meaning to give birth to. It means "The one who bore God" or "The God bearer."

Her body was so sacred. It was God's temple. Mary... simple, not the best at everything, teenage Mary... carried Jesus and sacrificed her body for the sake of my salvation... for the sake of your salvation.

"Those whose hearts are pure are temples of the Holy Spirit."
-St. Lucy

You and I, as women, have the same feminine body that God chose to use as His vehicle into our world. Let that sink in.

Wait, there's more.

As Baptized Christians and Catholics, we too are God-bearers. Not only are we made in the image and likeness of God, but when we're Baptized, we enter into the life of the Trinity and become members of God's family. Living a life in God's grace is to participate in His life, and to have Him living in you. Just as Mary physically brought Christ to this world through her body, we're called to bring Him spiritually to this world through ours.

St. Teresa of Avila once said,

> *"Christ has no body but yours, no hands, no feet on earth but yours. Yours are the eyes with which He looks Compassion on this world. Yours are the feet with which He walks to do good.*
> *Yours are the hands, with which He blesses all the world."*

This is a great prayer to read every day before you get dressed. It's a great reminder to hang in your room or tape onto your mirror.

Your body isn't something abominable and loathsome. Reject that lie.

God says to each of us, "you are precious in my eyes and honored, and I love you" (Isaiah 43:4). Mary was welcomed into God's life of grace early in order that we all could be welcomed into His life of grace. We have been redeemed and are therefore worthy of being God bearers. He has chosen each of us to bring His love into the world in a unique way. That's the mission we received by our Baptism.

If you see your body in this way, hopefully it takes on the sacredness that God intended it to have. We don't want to hate the instrument that God has chosen to use — our own bodies.

And by your body, I mean you. Another idea we have to change is the mindset that our body is something that is separate from us. God made each of us to be one being, made of a body and soul. *You* are a God-bearer, not just your body.

We have to change our thought patterns. Daughters need to hear they are beautiful from the most important man in their life — their father. If you never heard that you're beautiful from your dad or anyone else, you have to make the effort to re-wire your brain to believe this truth. That lack of affirmation can leave a hole in us that we try to fill with attention from other men, often resulting in promiscuity.

Your other Father (the one in heaven) wants to tell you how beautiful you are. He made the heavens and the earth, He made the galaxies of stars and the beautiful landscapes of the world, but it wasn't enough. *You* weren't there. It was lacking you. You've been in the mind of God forever. The same hands that created the stars, created you.

I am in awe of this simple truth.

Anytime I'm feeling like I can't handle everything that's going on, when I feel inadequate, and like I'll never be enough, I remember this: God made me purposefully and He's always there for me. Not only is He watching over us, but He longs to be intimately involved in every aspect of our day. All day He is caring about me, trying to show me His love. It's me who forgets that, who doesn't invite Him in, and who ends up being self-centered and unhappy, beating myself up for all the little things — like body image.

In re-wiring our brains, we have to take the simple truths about who we are and make the effort to remind ourselves of them constantly. It means replacing any negative self-talk (the mean things you tell yourself in your mind) with positive messages. Where has negativity ever gotten you anyway? You'll get so much further with loving yourself. If you can get to a place where you accept yourself however you are, victories and failures, you can move forward from there and continue to work on improving yourself and your health.

You can either limit or encourage yourself by what you believe about yourself. If you believe you can dig deep down in your heart and love your enemies, with God's grace you'll be able to. If you believe you are inadequate, you limit yourself to that quality.

What are the things you tell yourself? What is the soundtrack of your destructive thinking?

I tell myself that I'm not good enough in every aspect and area of my life. I tell myself that I'm not beautiful and that if I want to be happy I have to look more like her, her, and her. I went through a period of my life in college where I always said, "I suck at life." Yeah, a pretty depressing thing to hear in your head all the time. That only motivated me to feel bad about myself and lie down on my bed in misery instead of pursuing a full, healthy life.

First, you have to interrupt the "Negative Nancy" voice in your mind. Divert your attention. Tell yourself to stop thinking that way. Pray a "Hail Mary." Then, you need to challenge the things you're telling yourself. For me, when I said "I suck at life" I needed to challenge myself by asking, "Is that really true? Do you really fail at everything? No! Just because you occasionally mess up, that doesn't ever mean that you suck at life! What about that time you told Maureen not to buy those shoes? That was nice of you!"

The next time you tell yourself that you're ugly and fat, I dare you to challenge that by asking yourself if God makes mistakes. Does He make people who are less than what He sees as perfect? He's God. And when God creates something, He doesn't stop until it's exactly how He wants it.

You need to counter your negative statements with positive ones. Instead of saying "I'm not good enough" I have learned to say "I'm a loveable and capable person," and "I have many good qualities." Instead of "I'm not pretty enough" I look in the mirror and say "You're beautiful." I know it sounds funny and weird. If you want to say, "I'm beautiful and it's bizarre that I'm talking to myself" that's okay.

Try saying, "I love myself just the way I am."

Also, accept a compliment. We feel so inadequate and unworthy of praise because we still aren't happy with the number on the scale or the imperfections we see in the mirror. As you start replacing your negative thoughts, take note of how often someone tells you how great you are or how nice you look. I'm not saying post a "selfie" everyday looking for likes and comments from people you barely know, but from the people around you who love you. Don't dismiss their compliment either out loud or in your mind. Say "thank you" and mean it because they mean the compliment.

Once you're able to accept and love yourself, pursuing a healthier lifestyle comes naturally. Your body is a temple; you've got to treat it like one! Scripture tells us:

> *"Do you not know that your body is a temple of the holy Spirit within you, whom you have from God, and that you are not your own? For you have been purchased at a price. Therefore, glorify God in your body" (1 Corinthians 6:19-20).*

It takes a lot of work to counteract the message of the world that tells us that we're only as good as the size of our skinny jeans. No man's attention, or amount of Facebook 'likes,' or number on the scale will ever heal that distorted, negative message. You've got to do it yourself.

Our mothers play a big role in forming the attitude we have about our bodies. And do you know what Mary said?

"My soul proclaims the greatness of the Lord; my spirit rejoices in God my savior. For he has looked upon his handmaid's lowliness; behold, from now on all ages call me blessed. The Mighty One has done great things for me, and holy is his name" (Luke 1:46-49).

She knew what a blessing it was to be God's chosen one. Do you know what a blessing it is to be God's chosen daughter? He's chosen you for great things. Mary praised God for everything He had given her. Are you grateful for God's gifts to you? He's giving you them all day long. Mary knew how awesome she was and she was confident in that. She said, "All generations will call me blessed" (Luke 1:48). That's not proud, it's honest! You can be honest about your greatness. Take the time to affirm yourself. God has done great things for us. He gave you a body so you could share His love to every person you encounter.

Your mama Mary understands your struggle with body image; let her attitude rub off on you. Just as Mary sat in awe, holding her womb, and thanked God for making her body His dwelling place. Like Mary, honor your body too. God is with you and longs to help you understand how sacred your body is. Glorifying God in our bodies through our actions and attitudes begins with recognizing the truth of His presence with us. When you remind yourself of that truth, you will naturally begin to desire to honor Him with every decision, whether it involves a second bowl of ice cream, or how you love others with your body.

> "I understood that the greatest attribute of God is love and mercy."
>
> -St. Faustina

"The way to begin healing the wounds of the world is to treasure the Infant Christ in us; to be not the castle but the cradle of Christ; and, in rocking that cradle to the rhythm of love, to swing the whole world back into the beat of the Music of Eternal Life" (Caryll Houselander, Wood of the Cradle, Wood of the Cross).

Purity:
You Can't Have My V-Card

"I need to tell you something... " I whispered hesitantly, turning my face away from him as he leaned in to kiss me.

"Um, okay..." Ethan responded, sounding both worried and receptive at the same time. We had been seeing each other for about a month, which is long enough to know someone's favorite music and coffee order, but not long enough to trust them to fully understand your morals and boundaries. I wanted to make sure I was clear with him, so I took a deep breath and sent up a quick prayer for courage before telling him a very important fact about me.

"I'm not having sex until I'm married."

The words tumbled out of my mouth and I couldn't believe how simultaneously difficult and easy that was to say. It was easy to say because my whole life I had been committed to this ideal and had known, without a doubt in my mind, that my goal was to wait for marriage. But it was also incredibly difficult to say because:

a. I didn't know how Ethan would respond,
b. things were about to get really awkward and honest and raw, and
c. it's MUCH easier to not interrupt a kiss to stop and talk about where you stand on giant, moral life decisions.

It's like being at the fair and stopping in the middle of the smelly pig exhibit to discuss the morality of carnivore-ism. Who does that? Just go enjoy the Ferris Wheel.

Interrupting this would-be romantic moment with Ethan was seriously *the last thing* I wanted to do.

But there I was, putting it out on the line because I had to be sure he knew where I stood and where he wasn't going to lie — in my bed. To be totally honest with you, when I was telling Ethan that I wasn't going to have sex before marriage, I couldn't remember any of the reasons why this was a good idea morally. My mind went completely blank, and instead of telling him the lofty theological and psychological reasons that make perfect sense, all I could think of to say was "this is a choice I've made." I said the words that I knew I believed, but it was a 5 percent moment.

"Let us raise ourselves from our fall and not give up hope as long as we free ourselves from sin."

-St. Margaret of Cortona

Purity is important to me 95 percent of the time. For example, it was very easy for me to choose purity when a man in Paris asked me to live with him for two weeks ("...and don't worry I don't have a wife or girlfriend" he so kindly added). Yes, that really happened. After saying no, I couldn't walk away fast enough.

The other 5 percent is when I'm being tempted and my mind is saying, "purity is boring and outdated." Sin ALWAYS seems more fun than virtue when you're faced with a choice between the two. After the fact, not so much. But when everything in you is saying, "there's nothing wrong with this!" that should be a red flag that "there's something wrong with this!"

I've seen in my life and in other people's lives that when you follow the law of God, it leads to happiness, and when you deviate from the plan that He has for humanity, it brings unhappiness. I want to be happy.

Sex is a really big deal. You probably know that, but just to reaffirm this — it is a big deal. It's not "just" sex, it's part of who you are. It's not just something you do with your body because your body and soul can't be separated. You're one person, not a person with body parts.

St. Thomas Aquinas said that "to love is to will the good of another" (Summa Theologica I-II). This means that whether or not you "feel" like it, the way to love someone is to choose what's best for their soul. What's the greatest good in every situation? That's what you should be asking yourself when you love someone. The greatest good in regards to sex is to save it for its proper expression within the context of the Sacrament of Marriage where both people are totally committed to each other and can be open to children.

It's only with God's grace that I will to have the strength to wait until marriage when I can give myself fully to my spouse. I have to pray for that grace every day. I don't want to only give half of myself to someone. We were made for communion with another person in our bodies and in our souls.

I don't want to give my body to a guy — which is saying here's *all* of me — without being 100 percent committed to him within the Sacrament of Matrimony. God made sex for two purposes: babies and bonding. If you think about sex, it's obvious that it can accomplish two goals, to bring a couple closer to one another and to create children. The only proper context for those two purposes is within the Sacrament of Marriage. Sex is the super-glue of the soul and I don't want to be bonded to someone who can peace out at any moment. Just because you share thousands of text messages, inside jokes, or even your rent payment with someone, it doesn't mean they're going to stick around. I don't want to risk getting hurt like that, do you?

Abstaining from sex makes sense. It's really difficult and it's a sacrifice... but it makes sense and brings me peace. (God's plan has a funny way of being like that — logical and happy-inducing.)

The cool thing about sex is that it's incredibly holy (but don't look to Cosmo Magazine to tell you that). My older sister Mary Theresa taught me how sacred sex is. She got married when I was a teenager. It was during a time in my life when I had been learning about sex from conversations with my friends and from TV. After she was married, we began to talk more about sex, and our conversations about sex changed drastically from something "we don't talk about" to something awesome, holy, and sacramental.

If sex is so holy, such a beautiful reflection of the life-giving love of the trinity, then why was Mary a virgin her whole life?

Because the discipline of denying yourself something good for the sake of something even better makes you holy. We believe that from a young age Mary had committed herself to a life of chastity because she wanted to be totally God's. He was her beloved, and the most important person in her life.

Mary was confused when the Angel Gabriel said she would give birth to a son because Mary was committed to remaining pure for God. It's not possible for a virgin to give birth! But since when has God been limited by what's physically possible? Doing impossible things is His forte, His favorite, His cup of (figurative) tea.

Not only was Mary a virgin before Jesus was born, she also remained a virgin after He was born. She and Joseph experienced a union of their souls, that was better than the excitement of the union of the flesh. Their marriage was focused solely on God and in order to ensure that was the case all the time, in all areas of their lives, they chose to forego having sex.

Also, Mary was the spouse of the Holy Spirit. I feel like being the spouse of the Holy Spirit would come with some serious perks. On the top of my list of requests would be asking that my coffee doesn't get cold, that I don't suffer from allergies, and that I be privileged to enjoy some of the most spectacular sunrises — my favorite part of the day.

But even though Mary was sinless and was the spouse of the Holy Spirit, she was still human! And don't forget she still had an earthly spouse, St. Joseph, to throw into the equation.

Men and women are made with bodies that *want* to have sex. (Let's be honest, the world wouldn't last very long if people didn't enjoy procreating.) Mary and Joseph weren't any different. Like I've said before, being sinless and possessing great virtue doesn't mean life is easy. It means when the temptations and struggles came along, they overcame them with God's grace. Well at least Mary always overcame them, Joseph wasn't sinless.

Purity is incredibly difficult and in Mary we have a mom who understands. In St. Joseph we have an example of real manhood. Being a saint doesn't mean you're not tempted, it means you choose to control your body with the higher faculties of your soul, it means you allow your soul to "lead" your body and not the other way around.

They both had to work hard to protect this purity; it had to have been a struggle. I think that as the holy man he was, St. Joseph must have taken a big part in being the protector of their purity. This elevates him to "best man ever" status.

Please just think about this realistically. These two awesome, holy, young, attractive people were getting married to each other. I don't know if you've talked to any engaged couples but they're usually pretty excited for the wedding night. This is where hashtags within books would come in handy: #justsayin.

Mary was a young girl like you and I. She would have been excited about falling in love with Joseph. She was excited about her wedding dress! She dreamed about what her life with Joseph would be like.

I think that after the Angel Gabriel told Mary that she was to give birth by the power of the Holy Spirit, it became evident to her that she was the one prophesied in Isaiah 7:14 — the virgin who would give birth to a son. She had already made the choice to remain a virgin. God never forces His plan on us, we always have a choice.

And it was a choice she made over and over until the day she died. She was a perfect model of a life totally dedicated to God. That's why I ask her to pray for me and that I'll be strong in the face of temptations too; I need all the help I can get.

I bet you're wondering what happened when I told Ethan that I wasn't going to have sex before marriage. I wish that I could say he nodded understandably. I wish I could tell you that we talked about our mutual desire to pursue purity together and that we sat side by side and discussed what healthy, physical boundaries we should have in order to stay pure, but that was not how the conversation went.

When I revealed my counter-cultural lifestyle to him, he said, "so... are you okay with other stuff?" (This is another way of saying, "how far is too far" or "how much can I get away with?") It was obvious to me that this was someone who wanted to try and push boundaries and not work together with me to grow in virtue and pursue sainthood.

I deserve a man who is going to fight to protect my purity, not tell me repeatedly how difficult and frustrating it is that we can't "go all the way." I want a man like St. Joseph, and that's what I want for you too.

Regardless of how you've fallen in the past, purity is something that you can recommit to at any time, or hundreds of times if you need to.

There are countless people who, after having an encounter with Christ, have realized that they want to live purely. Sins against purity are serious sins that, when ignored, can change the course of your life completely. But, there is hope. Christ gave us the Sacrament of Reconciliation so that we can be reunited to Him. Sin separates us from God — sins against purity hurt our relationship with God. But, when we seek His forgiveness in the Sacrament, that relationship is restored.

When a young girl gets pregnant and the people around her gasp and whisper "I can't believe it, she was such a good girl" ... I cry a little on the inside. That's not fair. Good people can trip and fall and your goodness isn't dependent on what sins are in your past. Remaining a virgin is more difficult than finding a *Forever XXI* top that doesn't shrink in the wash, and if I'm able to stay pure from one day to the next it's only because I've been able to accept God's grace to be strong.

Once, one of my family members was telling me about someone I had known from high school who had gotten pregnant. She said, "That's what happens when you move far away from home and have boys over late at night." Actually... no. That's what can happen in *any* place, at *any* time, when you let your guard down.

St. Maximilian Kolbe put it perfectly when he said:

> *"Whenever you feel guilty, even if it is because you have consciously committed a sin, a serious sin, something you have kept doing many, many times, never let the devil deceive you by allowing him to discourage you. Whenever you feel guilty, offer all your guilt to the Immaculate, without analyzing it or examining it, as something that belongs to her... My beloved, may every fall, even if it is serious and habitual sin, always become for us a small step toward a higher degree of perfection. In fact, the only reason why the Immaculate permits us to fall is to cure us from our self-conceit, from our pride, to make us humble and thus make us docile to the divine graces" (Letter of Saint Maximilian Kolbe).*

If you've struggled with purity, or if you aren't a virgin anymore, I want to be sure you know that you're *not* "damaged goods," or less worthy of love. Don't let the devil convince you that the sins you've already repented (gone to Confession for) make you a bad person.

I was strong enough this time to tell a guy "no," but I don't have that guarantee for next time.

I hope the example of Mary and Joseph inspires you instead of discourages you. Ask them to pray with you the next time you're tempted to act impurely. If you can have the frame of mind to pause and offer an honest Hail Mary, or even a short plea for help, Christ *will* come to your aid in prayer. The other advice I can give you is that in the 95 percent of the time when purity seems like an awesome idea, pray for the grace to choose purity when it may be hard. Only good things happen when you decide to live a life of purity. When some ideal, virtue, or goal is tough to obtain, that usually means it's of high value and will only make you a better, stronger person.

The best advice I can give you is to be honest with any guys you start dating. If I was able to muster the courage to tell Ethan I wasn't having sex... you can too. It was hard for me to tell him, but it was so worth it.

When you stand up for what you believe in and the morals you want to live out, a guy can have one of two reactions. He will either say, "that's too difficult, why would I deny myself in that way?" He could be inspired to embrace the challenge (if he hasn't already) and become the protector and gentleman that he was made to be.

> "He loves, He hopes, He waits. Our Lord prefers to wait Himself for the sinner for years rather than keep us waiting an instant."
> -St. Maria Goretti

There's this quote I love from Archbishop Fulton Sheen that's on my refrigerator right now. Partly as a reminder to my two roommates and myself but also as a subtle way to let the guys who come through our house know what's expected of them. It says:

> *"When a man loves a woman, he has to become worthy of her. The higher her virtue, the more noble her character, the more devoted she is to truth, justice, goodness, the more a man has to*

aspire to be worthy of her. The history of civilization could actually be written in terms of the level of its women."

That's not to say that we women have an "upper hand" in relationships or that we are trying to manipulate men to act a certain way in order to be "worthy" of our affection. Not at all. (I think it could just as easily go the other way too if a woman needs to be held to a higher standard.) Fulton Sheen is simply saying that women have a power within them to inspire men to become better men.

"It is love alone that gives worth to all things."

-St. Teresa of Ávila

You and all your feminine wonder are so alluring that you can set the standard of how a man can and can't treat you. If you value your dignity enough to speak up for what you deserve, the right guy will fight for you.

And the others will peace out like Ethan. You deserve someone who wants to become a saint with you, not someone who you're dragging along behind you on the road to heaven. Ask St. Joseph to pray with you for your future vocation. If you're called to marriage, you'll be sure that St. Joseph is praying for that man. If you're called to the religious life, you can be sure he's praying for your strength to remain chaste. Your life isn't random and God's will is always being accomplished — even if it takes some time and you make some mistakes along the way.

Emotions:
I'm an Ugly Crier

So there's this stereotype about us women. People (okay fine, men) tend to see us as out-of-control, bathroom-floor-crying, box-of-chocolate-eating, plate-throwing, drama-queens-here-to-make-everyone-miserable.

I have a confession. I *may* have helped support this theory about us. So, from the bottom of my chocolate-loving heart I apologize and hereby promise that I have (mostly) amended my ways.

To make matters worse, I'm an ugly crier. I don't know how some girls manage to still look adorable while crying. Have you ever noticed that in movies? It's insane. Not me. I'm a blotchy-faced, red-eyed, snot-streaming, hyperventilating, hot mess. If there are any cute-criers out there, any secret skills you have and would like to share are more than welcome.

From the time I was young, I was dramatic about things. I grew up with my grandparents as my next-door neighbors. This was cool because they had cable, an endless supply of ice cream, doting hearts, and two horses. For a pre-teen *American Girl* books fan, this was a dream come true. All I had to do was step outside and my life was like a scene from the lives of the fictional characters I loved.

There came a time, however, when the horses became more work and money than they were worth. My grandparents decided to sell them. On the morning Buck and Domino were picked up by their new owners, I couldn't be in the way of the adults and vehicles. I ran up to my room to watch the commotion from my second story window. I knew that moment had the potential of being just like a scene from a book or movie, so I played it up. I dug down deep into my heart and found the shreds of sentimental attachment I had to those two horses (I had ridden them a few times and hated their smell). As the trailer was driving away, I forced some tears to come out of my stubbornly dry eyes. I made sure to wave and put my hand dramatically on the windowpane. Then, I wrote about it in my bedazzled pink journal equipped with a lock. (After the story about how I thought my wild chipmunk pet had become road kill. Apparently I had a thing about animals.)

Being emotional is all about reacting in the moment to what you're "feeling." For a lot of people it's not a time for rational thought processes or thinking things through. It's not a time to look at the facts or the pros and cons. It's time to let everyone know how you *feel*, and if anyone tells us it's wrong to *feel* that way... watch out.

Actually, it's not wrong to feel that way — whatever way it is that you're feeling right now. Emotions are not good or bad, they just are. Once we give ourselves permission to feel our emotions, we're free to live with much more self-awareness, and we give ourselves freedom to be authentic.

Who we are and how we express our emotions has a lot to do with how we were raised. Everyone has a different and unique family system that they grow up in and none of them are perfect. One of the things about my family is that we weren't very open about our emotions.

I remember one night at dinner my little sister was very hurt by something another family member had said to her earlier. We sat down for dinner in silence while tears were streaming down my sister's face. We started eating salad... silence... tears... awkward.

After awhile I was fed up with it and the "don't ask, don't tell" policy we had about emotions. I started asking what was wrong. I asked again and again, and then started volunteering options of what she could be upset about (like any annoying middle child would do). Finally it came out and there was a little confrontation among family members, but no resolution. I'm pretty sure someone left the table mad but at least we *acknowledged* the emotion!

That was just one instance where I rebelled though. My family rarely acknowledged feelings or confronted one another. Later, when I went to college, I still had this attitude that my emotions should be hidden and not shared with anyone. I was afraid that by sharing my emotions, I would become a "burden" to other people. So, with that way of thinking, I never shared my emotions.

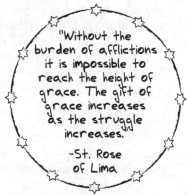

"Without the burden of afflictions it is impossible to reach the height of grace. The gift of grace increases as the struggle increases.

-St. Rose of Lima

Because of this extreme view on emotions, the first person to convince me I wasn't a burden to them received a full force avalanche of *everything* I was feeling. I went from one extreme to the other. The pendulum swung the opposite way and suddenly I was an emotional wreck about everything. One of my friends even lovingly nicknamed me "faucet" because I cried so much. True story. If I had a fight with my roommate: End of the world. Getting an 89 on a test? End of the world. No more rice krispie treats in the cafeteria? Why does God hate me?!?

I knew it wasn't good to bury all my feelings but letting them all out wasn't bringing me peace either. Trying to balance between both extremes was hard and I'm sure you've dealt with a similar situation at some point in your life.

I'm sure you've figured out by now that God made women to be more emotional than men. If we believe that God knows what He's doing (I still haven't figured out the 'why' behind volcanoes but whatever) then He must have created us this way for a reason and there's got to be a better way to live than being blown around in this hurricane of emotions... right?

Mary is a beautiful example of how we, as women, are meant to handle our emotions. She had them too! Mary cried about things (but I doubt she was an ugly crier). Maybe not about work, a movie, and a migraine like I did this past week, but she had her moments.

Not being able to find a warm room to give birth in — I can bet she might have shed a couple tears over that. How about when

Jesus was a young boy and she and Joseph realized He wasn't with them on their way back from the temple in Jerusalem? I can't even imagine how upset she must have been. It's a big deal to lose God. They searched for three agonizing days. I bet it was hard to not let their imaginations run wild with scenarios of what could have happened. Camel accidents were a real thing. (Side note: so many problems from the past could be solved with cell phones... "Jesus, where are you?" "BRB Mom, droppin' some mad wisdom @Temple.")

Finally they found Him. (My mind just exploded with the realization that they didn't look at the temple first, but after three days... as if they figured He would be hanging with friends, or exploring Jerusalem Aladdin-style.)

They enter the Temple and see Him all the way on the other side. Mary grabs Joseph's hand as they speed-walk towards Jesus (you don't run in the temple, obviously); a sigh of relief and frustration comes from both of them. And then, typical of my idea of who Mary was — so spunky and full of life — she is the first to interrupt the theological discussion and exclaim:

> *"'Son, why have you done this to us? Your father and I have been looking for you with **great anxiety.**' And he said to them, 'Why were you looking for me? Did you not know that I must be in my Father's house?' But they did not understand what he said to them. He went down with them and came to Nazareth, and was obedient to them; and **his mother kept all these things in her heart**" (Luke 2:48-51, emphasis added).*

Two things that I want to talk about: "great anxiety" and "she kept all these things in her heart."

Now I've been left behind places so I can relate to this story. One time I was left at a pizza restaurant and then not even two weeks later I was left at church. My parents were naturally worried about me, so I cannot imagine how Mary felt losing the Son of God!

I mean, any mother would freak out when their child is missing. Mary owned the fact that she was feeling a very strong emotion: anxiety. She didn't apologize for it or hide it. She also didn't let it control her. The passage doesn't say she went home and Jesus was grounded for 70 times 7 days. She didn't go home and hold a grudge or stay angry. Mary just dwelt on what had happened *in her heart*. She processed it with the Holy Spirit, not with her girlfriends around the village well.

She didn't let her emotions control her.

This is so key to understanding how to live peacefully as a woman. This gift of feeling emotions intensely doesn't have to be a curse. It's actually a blessing!

Women tend to be more interior and heart-centered than men are. It means we're more inclined to compassion, empathy, and understanding. Girls are more intuitive and sensitive. Sometimes our tears flow like Niagara Falls.

"Love the Virgin Mary. She is our tender confidant in difficulty. Mary is the mother who cannot ignore our requests."

-St. Gianna Beretta Molla

This sensitivity has the potential to cripple us. Unchecked by reason, emotions can spin out of control. Once they found Jesus, Mary did not need to be anxious or bitter. Reason told her that He was now safe, no harm had been done, and further drama over this episode was pointless.

A very wise priest-friend of mine once said, "When virtue goes up, drama goes down." A virtuous person is someone who seeks truth in every situation.

What's the truth that you need to speak to your emotions? Ask God to reveal it to you. He gave us sensitive hearts but He also gave us brilliant minds. It's time to use these two together.

What does that look like?

Well... I'm glad you figuratively asked.

It means that when you're upset over a break-up, you first give yourself permission to feel whatever emotion you're feeling. Then you speak truth to that emotion. You remind yourself that God has a plan for your life (Jeremiah 29:11) and He wants you to be happy (John 10:10). Yes, you should let yourself be sad over the loss of a relationship but that should be balanced by hope for the future and not exacerbated by extreme thinking such as "I'm always going to be alone" or irrational behavior like gossiping about your ex.

Having a sensitive heart means we're tuned in to other's problems. So what about if you're worried sick over a friend who is heading down a bad path in life? The wrong thing to do is to become over-involved and attempt to "save" your friend. You'll end up upset over every bad choice they make, sometimes blaming yourself for not doing more. Truth and reason say you are only in control of your own life and choices. You can pray for your friend, but their troubles shouldn't hold you back in your own life. Being worried is valid. Allowing your worry to bring you down and make you attempt to fix another person — not cool.

> "The truth does not change according to our ability to stomach it."
>
> -Flannery O'Connor

There are a hundred moments a day when we have the opportunity to speak truth to our emotions. I used to feel guilty for all my emotions but they are a huge blessing because they are a part of what makes me a woman. They're in my nature.

St. Thomas Aquinas said, "Grace builds upon nature." Whatever is in your nature is what God is going to use to make you a saint. Mary was a woman with emotions like you and me, but she surrendered everything to God.

I need to surrender my emotions to God (sometimes multiple times a day!) so that they can be used for His glory. You can use your feelings to learn where you need to grow in virtue. You can turn your emotions into actions for the greater good of someone else. If you're feeling sad because your friend just went through a break-up, use that emotion as a motivation to go cheer them up and do an act of charity. You can also use your emotions as a motivation to turn to God and find comfort in Him. When you're feeling upset, lonely, heartbroken, etc., that's an ideal time to find comfort in God.

One of my favorite Bible verses for times of suffering, especially emotional suffering, is Psalm 34:19:

"The Lord is close to the brokenhearted, saves those whose spirit is crushed."

That's God's promise to you — that you'll never be alone, no matter what you're going through or what you're feeling.

I have learned that I don't have to brush my emotions under the rug and I don't have to let them control me. There's power in having a sensitive heart, even if you're an ugly crier, and even if you feel a handful emotions from ecstatic happiness to infuriating anger... all within ten minutes.

Anger:
She Said WHAT?

Girls are dainty. They wear pink and sparkly earrings, and wear vintage dresses. Preferably all at the same time.

Girls are polite. A girl should never make a scene unless it's because she's that one girl that stuns the entire room with her beauty and grace.

Girls are composed. They don't lose their temper or get angry. They don't express all of their emotions for the sake of "keeping the peace."

How do you feel about being put into that box? Yeah, I kind of hate it too. Vehemently. While there's nothing particularly wrong with those things, and they may all have their place (on prom day!), we are more than that stereotype.

I've punched walls. I've screamed into pillows. I've ran four miles (one mile in tears) fueled by an emotion raging inside me. I have pages in my journal of multiple angry rants. I've burst through my front door, thrown myself on the couch and complained about my day (which is awkward if there are people in the living room trying to watch a movie). Not saying all these are healthy but they're real and I'm working on it. That's the beauty of being on the road to sainthood, I'm a "work in progress" and sometimes I'm "that one girl" who doesn't have it all together.

After expressing those angry emotions, I've felt very, very guilty. "I need to get myself together," I would think. "Stop being so childish Christina. Grow up. Get over it. You shouldn't feel this way."

The attitude that I grew up with was that maintaining a composed, beautiful exterior was more important than giving myself permission to feel what was going on in my heart. I felt that I should always bury any angry feelings and wait for them to go away. (Which just to be clear, doesn't ever happen. You can bottle up your emotions but they will eventually explode.)

I was a slave to the "Law of Shoulds." An unspoken law of how everyone "should" act and feel according to... I have no idea whom. There's a voice in my head, separate from my conscience (which is and always will be a good barometer of how to act according to God's commandments), that told me what I should be feeling, how I should respond to those feelings, and when I should feel guilty for expressing a certain emotion — especially anger.

The "Law of Shoulds" is what keeps us from accepting ourselves and other people without judgment. It makes you negative and critical because you believe there's this standard or expectation that everyone "should" follow... but how is everyone supposed to know that?

You know when you're in grade school and you learn all the rules of the English language, like when "i" goes before "e" and what a helping verb is? I think along with that it'd be awesome to incorporate a rule that says "should" and "feel" can never go in the same sentence.

Remember, emotions aren't good or bad, they just are and we have to listen to what we're feeling. I want to focus on this one emotion because I've been thinking about it a lot in relation to Mary.

Did you know that it's okay to be angry?

What if Mary got angry sometimes? Feeling anger isn't a sin. Jesus experienced righteous anger in the temple that day when He overturned a bunch of tables that people were using to

"Dear Blessed Mother, lend me your heart. I look for it each day to pour my troubles into."

-St. Gemma Galgani

buy and sell things. It was an offense against the sacredness of the temple and Jesus had a right to feel anger and express it appropriately (see John 2:14-15). Lashing out at another unjustly, gossiping, or slandering another person because of anger would be sinful.

I love imagining Mary as a feisty, passionate, full-of-life young woman. Why wouldn't she be? Since God wants us to be fully alive, wouldn't He choose a mother that was too? We so often reduce the Blessed Mother to a statue or a beautiful, somber woman standing in the clouds as queen over heaven, but she had a full life and a full range of emotions, including anger.

Anger swells up in us when we perceive that we have been misused or mistreated. It's a natural response that's a signal to help us identify how we deserve to be treated by others and what kind of boundaries are healthy.

For example, I used to get very angry when my little sister would throw pens and pencils at me from across the room. Yes, she is younger than me; however, she has a wicked good throwing arm, and combined with her impeccable aim, I was left rather helpless. I used my anger in those moments to lash out at her verbally, manipulating her to do something for me or else I would get her in trouble with our mom.

Not something I'm proud of. I did not deserve to have pointy objects thrown at me and my anger was just, but how I handled it was not.

When I think about Mary and anger, I can't help but think of how hard it must have been for her to be a young, unwed, and pregnant teenager. If you think people give teen moms the stink eye today, just imagine what Mary would have undergone back in her day. She could have been stoned to death!

Things can be all nice when you're sitting alone in prayer, but eventually you have to go out and face the rest of the world. Saying "yes" to the Angel Gabriel and to the Incarnation was already "greatly troubling" and confusing. Now imagine her telling her parents. Not to mention that her friends would have begun to notice her growing belly and the women would have started whispering about her at the well.

Don't you think Mary probably got a lot of dirty looks? Maybe even some nasty comments? Don't you think she would have been called names by the people in Nazareth? She didn't deserve any of it but what was she supposed to say?

"I'm pregnant by the grace of the Holy Spirit."

"An angel came to me and told me I was going to bear the Son of God."

"I'm still a virgin!"

She would have sounded crazy!

She had nothing to do but turn to God with her frustration and anger. Notice I didn't say turn *at* God in anger, but turn *to* Him. When you're defenseless against someone (or a group of people) who is spreading rumors and bad-mouthing you, anger is a natural response. It's like if you put your hand on a hot stove. The physical pain you feel alerts you to the fact that um, hello, you're going to get very hurt if you don't adjust your hand placement as soon as possible. The pain is a red flag that helps protect us.

Feeling angry is the same. The emotional pain raises up in us the realization of what we deserve and the standard by which we want to be treated, and therefore, by which we need to treat others.

"Nothing is far from God."

-St. Monica

There was a point in my life where a girl was spreading rumors about me to my friends. She was attacking my character and my good name and trying to turn other people against me. It really hurt me. I didn't know what to do. I felt helpless and I was angry.

The only comfort I had was my confidence in the fact that she was wrong. Only God and I knew what was in my heart and there was nothing I could do to prove myself to everyone else. It felt like me against the world.

God doesn't like it when we get hurt. He would never wish that upon us. He would have loved it if all the people around Mary were compassionate and loving, regardless of what her situation was. He would love it if girl-drama were non-existent. (So would a lot of us I'm quite certain.)

God wants to be there for us in everything — even our anger. I'm sure that when the Blessed Mother was whispered about and isolated because she was "that one girl that was pregnant," she would have sought comfort in God alone. She had a right to be angry because she didn't deserve to be treated poorly. I'm sure she cried about it. Like my situation with the girl spreading rumors about me, Mary's only consolation was that she and God knew her divine secret and that she was as pure as the day she was born. That was the truth, no matter if no one knew it.

Don't forget that for every emotion we feel, we have to take the opportunity to speak truth into the situation. When you're angry, you have to ask yourself if the anger is rational or irrational. When my little (11-year-old) sister threw stuff at me, I had rational anger. If a 2-year-old started throwing things at me because they didn't know better, it would be irrational for me to get angry. When you're fired from a job because you shoplifted merchandise, you don't have the right to be angry. If you get fired from a job because someone accused you of shoplifting something that you didn't — you absolutely have a right to be angry. Own your anger.

Then, do something with it. Use it as a catalyst for change. Resolve to always find out all the facts before assuming something unkind about another person. Channel your anger into a rosary novena for that person... or channel it into a really great workout. Try to anticipate situations or people that often make you angry and prepare for it mentally. When you feel yourself starting to get angry, don't let it spin out of control before you deal with it. You don't have to wait until you lose your temper to admit that you feel angry.

Invite God into your anger; He's got this very calming personality, you know.

When I know that I need to just sit with God in prayer, I find it so helpful to visualize Jesus and myself sitting together somewhere. If you can, go to a church and sit and pray, knowing that Jesus is right beside you. If you can't get to a church, you can imagine sitting with Jesus. Just be there with Him. Allow His presence to calm you down. Let His truth wash away the lies, and allow His love to heal the hurt that others have caused you. Open up your Bible and ask God to speak to you. His words bring healing.

The thing about being a girl is that it's impossible to be a healthy, whole person and to have some emotions be taboo. Remember, emotions aren't good or bad. We live in a very broken, very sinful, and very painful world. People are going to hurt you and you'll hurt yourself trying to suppress any anger. Be careful in how you express it, but get it out and move on.

My little sister doesn't throw things at me anymore, my true friends stayed by my side, and I knew the rumors about me weren't true. Not to mention, "that one girl in Nazareth that got pregnant" went on to be the Queen of heaven. So epic win in all areas. You'll be okay too.

friendship:
My Gift to You

You know who I hope you can feel safe expressing your emotions with? Your friends. Good friendships can be one of God's greatest gifts. I don't know what I would do without my friends.

I love how the only recorded friendship of Mary is her friendship with her cousin Elizabeth. When the Angel Gabriel appeared to Mary, he told her that Elizabeth was also pregnant and already six months at that! Word sure traveled slowly. If Mary didn't even know that Elizabeth was miraculously pregnant even though she was so old, I bet Elizabeth didn't get a chance to hear that Mary was coming to visit her.

Imagine Elizabeth as she heard a knock on the door and had to heave herself out of her chair in the kitchen where she was trying to get dinner prepared. Everything is more difficult when you're pregnant, especially at her age, and she may have been feeling pretty discouraged about her housework.

"I'm coming," she said as she gathered up the laundry strewn around the room as quickly as her old, pregnant body would allow her to move. "I wish I had put this away earlier... What if this is someone who wants to stay and chat? What if I have to entertain someone for dinner? God help me," she murmured as she swung open the door.

"Elizabeth!" Mary exclaimed. It was all she could get out before they warmly embraced. It had been so long since they had seen each other. Elizabeth immediately knew (through the power of the Holy Spirit) that her sweet, young, and holy cousin was the chosen one who was carrying the Savior of the World. Boy, would they have a lot to talk about.

Do you notice how Mary's first action after the Incarnation was to go out and bring Christ's presence to someone else... with urgency? The Gospel literally says that she traveled "in haste" (Luke 1:39). That's what God does in us. Full of the Holy Spirit, we can't help but go out and bring His love to someone else and to do it *immediately*!

You know that feeling when you're so excited about something that you can't wait to tell someone else? I love going to Confession at a particular church where both of the priests, through God's grace, are gifted with being so kind, loving, and helpful in the Sacrament of Reconciliation. My friend Jessie even nicknamed one of the priests we go to regularly for Confession "Fr. Awesome" because we didn't know his name and every single Confession was... without a doubt, you guessed it... *awesome*. I don't want to have to wait in a longer confession line, but I can't help but want to tell everyone that they should go to Confession at that parish because of how much it has blessed me.

God's grace compels us forward and outward. Venerable Archbishop Fulton Sheen wrote, "Mary, 'went with all haste'; she is always in a hurry to do good. With deliberate speed she becomes the first nurse of Christian civilization" (*World's First Love*).

Mary was other-centered, not self-centered. Her act of friendship was a self-gift. After Jesus was conceived in her womb, she couldn't stay home and keep the Savior all to herself. "There is nothing Mary has that is for herself alone — not even her Son. Before He is born, her Son belongs to others" (Venerable Archbishop Fulton Sheen, *World's First Love*).

All friendship is a gift. That's the only healthy way to look at it. It's not a relationship where one person has power over the other. It's not two people who "owe" each other something. It's not a relationship of necessity; you don't "need" one another. It's a gift — one heart to another.

God made us in His image and likeness (Genesis 1:26-27). So that means that we are most ourselves, and therefore, the happiest when we are most like Him. That's why virtue is so rewarding. By being patient and loving, we're being like God. By being like God we're being fully human and alive.

And who is God? He is a communion of three persons: Father, Son, and Holy Spirit. God is love (1 John 4:8). He is a constant giving and receiving of love. So that's what we were made for too! Heaven is the ultimate communion (with God) that we will experience. Marriage and a person's communion with their spouse is a foreshadowing of the communion with God in heaven. Celibacy is a communion with God that also looks forward to heaven. And friendship is a unique way to experience this communion and self-gift with another person in a less intimate way.

Don't you love having friends? It brings so much joy into my life to give the gift of my heart and my friendship to another person.

However, only *healthy* friendships bring this kind of joy. People can either drag you down and wear you out, or inspire and uplift you. Having the ability to find and be a good friend can be the difference between happiness and unhappiness. There is another quote by Venerable Archbishop Fulton Sheen that echoes this truth: "Mary, 'went with all haste'; she is always in a hurry to do good. With deliberate speed she becomes the first nurse of Christian civilization" (*World's First Love*).

In Mary's friendship with Elizabeth, we see her reaching out to help her. A true friendship is helpful. If you remember anything I say about friendship, remember this — true friendship is helpful. And I mean helpful in multiple ways — a true friend is someone who helps you to be a better, holier person and who helps you get closer to God and others. If they can help you pick out the perfect outfit for a date and also paint the fingernails on your right hand — that's an awesome bonus.

"One must see God in everyone."

-St. Catherine Labouré

Now, no one is perfect (we've been over this). One of the secrets to friendship is being okay with the fact that both of you will sometimes make mistakes. Imperfect people make for imperfect relationships. In friendship there will be disagreements, but confrontation doesn't have to be disastrous or scary because in a healthy friendship both people understand that good communication is key. True friends accept you for who you are and where you're at in life, no matter what. That's what unconditional love is and that's how Mary and Elizabeth's relationship was. Mary accepted Elizabeth all the years and years that she was barren while everyone else thought it was because she was sinful and God was punishing her. Elizabeth accepted Mary when she was young, pregnant, and unmarried. They trusted each other and accepted one another with love. That's a true friend.

There are two words that have changed how I act in all of my friendships: boundaries and expectations.

Good friends have healthy boundaries. A boundary is knowing where you end and another person begins — what is theirs versus what is yours. It means you remember that you have the power to say "no" sometimes. "No, I'm not doing your homework for you." "No, I can't come over right now because I want to workout." "No, I can't drop everything to help you because I have my own responsibilities." You don't have to please other people. You don't "owe" anyone anything, and taking care of yourself means understanding your right to say no. It's tricky because sometimes you have to say no to good things like having a deep, late-night conversation for the sake of something more important like getting a decent amount of sleep at night.

If you want to be there for someone else, you have to be a healthy, whole person yourself. That takes time and it means you have to have a boundary about what you can and can't do.

Expectations in friendship are important because expectations that aren't communicated can lead to fights, hurt feelings, or bitterness. If you expect that your friend is going to eat lunch with you at school every day but don't communicate that and then they don't. What happens? It can be easy to assume that they don't like you or that they don't want to be around you, but more than likely, those assumptions are not true. Since friendship is a gift from one person to the other, it's hard to have a lot of specific expectations. No one owes each other anything. Remember, there is no "Law of Shoulds."

If you want to see your BFF for coffee every weekend, communicate that expectation.

Don't use friendship to fill a void inside you. I know how easy it is to do that. God made each of us with a God-shaped hole in our hearts, and if we don't allow Him to be our everything, we're left trying to fill that space with friends, boys, food, shopping, alcohol, obsessions, or any other number of things.

A healthy friendship is one that helps you to become a better person. Jesus said "You know a tree by its fruit. A good tree produces good fruit" (Matthew 7:17-20). Are your friendships producing good fruit? Do you surround yourself with friends that help you grow as a person?

> "I alone cannot change the world, but I can cast a stone across the waters to create many ripples."
>
> -Bl. Teresa of Calcutta

Mary's sinless and virtuous nature was an inspiration and an example to Elizabeth. Likewise, Elizabeth, who was a lot older than Mary, had a lot of life wisdom to share with her younger cousin. They were walking the road to heaven together. Can you say that about you and your friends?

Is it just as natural to go to Mass together as it is to go to the mall together? Can you pray a rosary together just as easily as talk about a movie you just saw? Do your friends respect your morals and beliefs, or do they constantly try to challenge them? We can't get to heaven alone, we have to support and help each other.

There are countless saints who became saints next to their best friend — like Saints Perpetua and Felicity, Ignatius of Loyola and Francis Xavier, or Francis and Clare.

My best friend in grade school was a girl named Kelsey. As we grew up, our friendship began to be frustrating to me. I felt like I was maturing and beginning to care about deeper things but I was leaving her behind. When we hung out together, I felt as though I had to take a step back in my maturity to talk at Kelsey's level and laugh about the things she laughed about. We didn't share the same faith. We didn't go to the same school. The friendship wasn't helping me to be a better person, so I let it die out. I felt really guilty about that for a couple years, but came to understand that some friendships are only meant for a short time in our lives. People come and go, and that's okay.

Nothing against Kelsey, I have no bad feelings towards her and I hope her life is going great. It's not bad to be exclusive about the people you let into your inner circle. I don't mean cliquey, mean-girl-type, inner circle. We should always be trying to be charitable to everyone around us, but those friends who you share the gift of yourself with need to be carefully chosen over time.

When you meet someone new it can tend to be really exciting and it's tempting to want to jump into a close friendship even though you barely know them. Sure, you both love the Bieber-Boy and your favorite saint is St. Thérèse, but it's good to take your time. It can take years to know who a person really is.

There's a really important distinction about friendship that I have to make here. We have to be vigilant that being "other-centered" and making a self-gift to others doesn't come at a personal cost. Just because Mary went to Elizabeth's house to help her out doesn't mean she would have ceased caring for herself. This is where boundaries come in.

Mary was carrying God within her; she had to take really good care of herself. She had to maintain her prayer life and stay connected to the One whom her life revolved around — God. All of her attention was absolutely not focused on pleasing Elizabeth, getting Elizabeth's attention and approval, or on Elizabeth's wants, needs, feelings, and opinions.

Helping someone is different from controlling someone or allowing them to control you. It's very easy to slip into an unhealthy pattern where we feel like we need our friends to validate our actions and who we are. We can also let them have too much control over our emotional well-being. Do you ever find yourself falling apart and having a bad day because your friend is upset with you, or you're upset about something they did? That's not a good place to be.

Friends are supposed to be on an even plane with one another, not one friend with more power and control over the other.

When I was in high school, I was really close to a girl named Morgan. We both worked at the local library and spent hours side by side, shelving books, laughing, and talking about life. (Which of course means mostly talking about boys.) Naturally, over the three years we worked together, we grew very close. She was a very faithful Jehovah's Witness and often our conversations came around to the differences in our beliefs. I'd lie if I said I didn't want to try and convert her, and maybe she was trying to convert me too — I don't know. But our differences didn't define our friendship, they were just a facet of who we were. We were just two girls sharing their lives with one another.

One night in October, I came into work and found out that her grandmother had died suddenly in a car accident. She was devastated and I didn't know what to do. I felt so useless as a friend. There's not much you can do to comfort someone who's grieving; it's a painful process they have to go through themselves. The only thing I could think of to say was "I'm so sorry."

When I was 12 years old I lost one of my best friends in a tragic car accident. I was at an amusement park with a group of people from church when I found out. I was so shocked I couldn't even cry. The priest who was with us came right over to me and told me everything he could to comfort me — that she was in heaven with Jesus and Mary, that she was so happy now, and that one day we would see her again.

I couldn't say that to Morgan because that's not what she believed according to her religion. She didn't have any of those comforting thoughts because to her, nothing happened after death. She didn't know where her grandma was now. She didn't believe her grandma was happy in heaven with Jesus and Mary.

We were putting away books together and ironically, we came across a Christian book about heaven. Both of us stared at it awkwardly, knowing what the other was thinking. I told Morgan it was difficult for me to know what to say when I know she didn't believe her grandma's soul was in a better place. She floundered with what to say and admitted that she was confused and so doubtful about what actually happens after a person dies.

Morgan began to cry and so did I. Both of us standing there in the non-fiction aisle, wanting to see eye to eye, desiring to understand the truth about life after death, but ultimately helpless to each other because she was a faithful Jehovah's Witness, and I a faithful Catholic — two religions that are very opposed.

Although our religions were very different, I am thankful that I was able to share in that moment with her. I felt her pain, and as her friend, I wanted her to find healing. Christ calls us to love others, regardless of their religion or beliefs. I felt a lot of empathy for her because I understood her pain; I had experienced losing someone close to me too.

But, I took it too far. Although I never said this to her, I was frustrated with her. Frustrated that she didn't believe in heaven. Frustrated that I felt stuck. I felt that somehow I had to fix it.

I left work that night and drove to adoration, my heart heavy and tears streaming down my face because I wanted something so badly for Morgan that she didn't want for herself: salvation within the Church. I was worried about her soul and frustrated I couldn't do more for her.

So, I overreacted and let my emotions get carried away. I wanted to save Morgan, but whether she believed in Him or not, she already had a Savior, and His name is Jesus Christ. Jesus is more concerned with her salvation than I ever could be. I was trying to be helpful to her and help her see the truth. However, it came at the expense of my own peace, which isn't what God wants. My friendship with Morgan could only ever go so deep because we didn't share the same beliefs. We could laugh about the boys in our lives but could never gush over how wonderful the presence of Christ in the Eucharist is in our lives. She could only help me grow holier as a person to a certain degree because our lives were centered around very different faiths.

Scripture says, "a faithful friend is a sturdy shelter, he who finds one finds a treasure" (Sirach 6:14). I think you could look at that verse in two ways. It could mean a faithful friend, someone who is always there for you. Or it could be a faithful friend as in someone who's faithful to God and is trying to get to heaven. There's a big difference. That doesn't mean people of other religions can't be wonderful friends. That's absolutely not true. I'm simply saying that besides having friends from different walks of life, we also need people in our lives who are going to help encourage us to be saints and who are walking the same road to heaven.

"Kind words can be short and easy to speak, but their echoes are truly endless."

-Bl. Teresa of Calcutta

I love Morgan so much, but she's not my "Elizabeth" and she can never be while we have such different religions. That doesn't mean we can't be friends, it's just a limited friendship.

I don't know what kind of friends you have, but I challenge you to think about your friendships critically. Hold them up to the light of Mary and Elizabeth, how do they compare? Ask the Blessed Mother to teach you how to be a good friend and teach you how to bring Christ to others. If you ask her to pray that you find good friends, she will ask her Son to bring you friends that help you be a better, holier, and more loving person.

God wants you to be happy, He wants you to have good friends and to be a good friend. Friendships are like the sprinkles on the cupcake of life. It makes something that, honestly can be pretty ordinary and boring... extraordinary.

Daily Life:
This is Boring

Every day I wake up around 5:15 am. Yes, it is painful. My alarm clock has four legs and is named Riley. We go outside and exercise (love/hate relationship with this part) while the sun rises (only a love relationship here, it's my favorite part of the day). Then, I eat breakfast, drink coffee, and get ready for work. The worst part of my morning is blow drying my massive mane. Ugh, it takes *for-ev-er*. Last year I went through a very serious phase when I wanted to get dread locks. Not ready for the commitment of dreads though, so I gave up that wish.

Then I drive to morning Mass and then to work, and 89 percent of the time I listen to the exact same playlist on my iPod. (Routine, gotta love it. Thanks Mom!) I eat lunch at noon which is usually something that can go inside a corn tortilla (you'd be surprised how versatile those are) because I'm gluten and dairy free (not by choice, I didn't choose the GF lifestyle, the GF lifestyle chose me). At 3:00 pm myself and two of my co-workers have a piece of chocolate to make the afternoon more bearable. I leave work around five-ish, and if I have no errands, I go home to feed the hungry, hungry animal and crash on the couch.

Sometimes I'll think about doing something social... so, I update my Facebook status. I try to relax and then I go to bed really, old-ladyish early because every day I wake up around 5:15 am. My alarm clock has four legs... (right, already said that).

It goes round and round, monotonous like a merry-go-round. Of course, there are things that break it up, like a mid-week Bible study, and the times I don't just think about being social but actually go hang out with my friends or go out on a date.

So often, the reality is that life can get kind of boring. Most of us aren't called to go on life-long, exciting mission trips to foreign countries. Most of us aren't going to be asked to be a martyr for our faith.

I love thinking about the day-to-day life of the Holy Family. They spent 30 years living first in Egypt and then in Nazareth together before Jesus' public ministry of preaching and healing began. Thirty years. We know so little about that time. One thing's for sure, St. Joseph didn't tell us a lot about it.

What was it like? Probably pretty routine and monotonous, especially for Mary. Joseph and Jesus were carpenters, so they had that work which was rewarding and challenging. They probably always had new projects to be working on. I'm sure Mary took great care of her home. She did the baking and cleaned all their dusty clothes. She went to the well to get water. She was friends with the other women in her town, probably going to visit the home-bound often, and taking food to the beggars. She was faithful in prayer. She brought Joseph and Jesus water on the hottest days.

In other words, her day was full (for 30 years) of a lot of tasks that can be very boring, monotonous and *seem* like they have no meaning. Things aren't always what they seem. It may seem like some days are pointless, but actually, nothing is pointless in God's eyes. There are countless, ordinary people who became saints by being faithful in all the little things. St. Thérèse of Lisieux was so boring that when she was dying her fellow religious sisters were agonizing about what they would write about her in her obituary (*The Context of Holiness*). They had nothing to say about her! However, she became the patron saint of missions and only left France like once, and not to go on a mission trip!

You don't have to be a foreign missionary to spread the Gospel. Your mission field is on the other side of your bedroom door, in your kitchen, living room, and hallway. Your family needs you to love them radically. The people in your school need you to be Christ to them. The stranger on the street desperately needs someone to smile at them today.

The thing is, even though the things around us might be the same old, same old, the Lord wants to constantly work in our hearts to bring us into a closer relationship with Him and closer to heaven. If Mary's quiet life at home taught us anything, it's that sometimes God's will for us is to be faithful in the little things and to show our love for Him in the boring-ness.

Holiness and your "spiritual life" aren't something separate from your day-to-day life. Everything you struggle with, all your interactions with other people, all the things you do or don't do, that is the context in which you become holy.

One of my favorite authors, Marc Foley, said,

> *"The trials and tragedies of life, the fears and conflicts of the human heart are not obstacles to growth in holiness but the stage upon which the drama of holiness unfolds" (The Context of Holiness, 141).*

That means whatever you struggle with, that's what God is going to use to make you a saint. Don't hate yourself for being worried about your future, that is a reason to lean on God. Don't beat yourself up for your sins, it's a chance to experience the mercy of God. Your weaknesses are your strengths, they are what force you to turn to God (if you know to turn to God, of course).

Becoming holy is all about seeing things through the lens of "forever." Today won't happen again, so how will you make it count? What little acts of love and sacrifice will you offer to God? What will cause you to pray without ceasing today? Impatience? Anger? An annoying family member? What fear or insecurity will make you hide within Christ's arms today? Don't apologize for that insecurity, just go to Christ.

"I shall love You, I shall love You always; when day breaks, when evening turns into night, at every hour, at every moment; I shall love You always, always, always."

-St. Gemma Galgani

Happiness is found in doing the will of God. The Creator intimately knows His creation. He knows what will make you the happiest— and it's not owning the newest iPhone. It's definitely not in chasing after a boy's attention either. Sometimes I think happiness is the perfect cup of coffee, but then it's gone and I'm back to square one.

I'm about to make one part of God's will very, very easy for you – He wants you to take good care of yourself in your daily life. I have a problem with all the emphasis in Christian circles on setting ourselves aside for the good of our brothers and sisters in Christ because it often ends with a total loss of "self." If we're constantly giving, giving, giving and only focused on sacrificing our needs for other people then we end up losing ourselves in the process. Read this brilliant quote from St. Bernard of Clairvaux; this is exactly what I'm talking about!

> *"The man who is wise, therefore, will see his life as more like a reservoir than a canal. The canal simultaneously pours out what it receives; the reservoir retains the water till it is filled, then discharges the overflow without loss to itself [...] Today there are many in the Church who act like canals, the reservoirs are far too rare [...] You too must learn to await this fullness before pouring out your gifts, do not try to be more generous than God" (Sermons on the Song of Songs).*

I'm not saying that self-sacrifice isn't good, it's absolutely necessary. But dying to self so that Christ can live in us doesn't mean running yourself dry and exhausted in the process. Sacrifice does not mean losing who you are.

There has to be a healthy balance. God created each of us with a lot of needs. You need good relationships in your life. You need to eat good food. You need to move. You need to relax. You need to have accomplishments. You need support and affection. You need to express your feelings. You need freedom and boundaries. You need to have time for fun. You need to have a full life and all of these things are part of a full, healthy life. In fact, they're so important that sometimes it's better for you to say no to a day of volunteer work in order to spend time with your family and friends.

You can't give what you don't have. If you're empty inside, what do you have to share with others to enhance their life? If you're not connecting to God in prayer, how can you bring His love to other people? You can't over-spiritualize your life and say that God will make up for everything you're not doing for yourself. God's grace is amazing (I learned that in a song) but it doesn't take the place of you taking care of yourself. God isn't going to turn those cookies into broccoli in your stomach.

My wonderful mom likes to remind me of that saying, "God helps those who help themselves." He gave us the capability to take care of ourselves. He gave you a brain and you're doing a disservice to Him and to your brothers and sisters if you don't use it. You can't sit around and wait for a job offer to come in the mail without applying for jobs. You can't sit in your living room watching TV every day and expect God to place a man in front of you to start dating. You can't complain about not knowing what God wants for your life if you don't spend time in silent prayer every day. God wants to mold you but you have to give Him something to work with. He can work miracles but He wants to work in little, mundane, human ways because it increases our faith in Him. (And we all need that.)

There are two ways I can look at my "boring" day. The first way is to look at it like it's a burden and incredibly annoying. The other option for looking at my day goes a little something like this:

Every day I wake up around 5:15 am. Yes, it is painful so I offer it up for the souls in purgatory. My dog and I go outside and exercise (another opportunity to sacrifice as I sweat a small pond and my muscles ache) while the sun rises (one of the ways God romances my heart).

Then I eat breakfast, drink coffee, and get ready for work. The worst part of that is blow drying my massive mane. I try to practice patience. Sometimes I fail but I offer that meager effort to God as well. I actually have thought about this a lot and when I get to heaven I want to be the patron saint of impatient girls doing their hair. I don't think that patronage has been claimed yet. Now you know my secret! Don't take it if you get to heaven first, okay? This is binding contract right here.

"Without love, deeds, even the most brilliant, count as nothing."

-St. Thérèse of Lisieux

Then I drive to morning Mass (and pray for you, for my day, and for all the intentions on my heart) and then to work (where I learn to submit to God's will). I eat lunch at noon which is usually something that can go inside a corn tortilla. I thank God that I have food to eat, regardless if it's not nearly as tasty as the gluten-ous and dairy-full food that everyone else is eating. I leave work around five-ish and if I have no errands I go home, feed the hungry, hungry animal and crash on the couch (because I know my limits and after a day of work I need to recharge).

If you can't choose to be holy in your daily life, you won't be able to be holy in heroic situations. Mary's life was spent doing God's will faithfully in the little things so that when the big things came around, like the Incarnation, or Jesus' passion and death, she didn't sway in her resolve to follow God's will.

You might feel like a nobody, like that one girl that no one notices — but heaven is full of nobodies. There were thousands of people around Mary who had no idea who she was. Not so much anymore.

Suffering:
It's No Accident

I'm not going to pretend I have the answer to help you avoid suffering for your whole life. I'm also not going to pretend that I have all the answers to make your suffering better.

Suffering is never easy. In fact, it's very, very difficult. All of it. All the time. (Now doesn't that make you want to read on?)

Sickness, death, divorce, abuse, addictions, natural disasters, bullying, heartache… these things are no bowl of Lucky Charms.

I was once in a car accident. I was on my way to Mass, and I was going through an intersection when I was hit full speed on my passenger side. My less-than-small car (that's my way of not telling you outright that I was driving a mini-van) went spinning and bouncing around the road, hitting two other cars before I came to a stop on the sidewalk.

The instant I stopped moving, my whole being freaked out. I began shaking, screaming, and sobbing. An older man appeared at my shattered window and reached through to hold my hand. I locked eyes with him, squeezed his hand, and nodded as he told me everything was going to be okay.

But when? When was it going to be okay?

Getting lifted out of my window and surveying the intersection with metal and glass all over the place from the four cars involved, and seeing police and EMT's running around, things did not look okay. Crying on the phone, crying on my friend's shoulder, crying by myself while lying on the couch — I didn't feel okay.

The pain in my body only got worse during the hours after the accident. My mind wasn't helping either, with every horrific sight and sound on instant replay. The silence before the impact, the fear, the sound of the crash, the spinning, the bouncing, the airbags, the smoke, the confusion, the pain… all of it like a terrible nightmare that I couldn't shake.

Except this time it was real. And I was not okay.

My first reaction in these types of situations is almost always anger. Why me? Why now, God? How could You let this happen? I'm a good person, why should I be the one who can't walk without catching my breath in pain? I have work to do. I don't have time to waste a week recovering on the couch. I can't afford to buy name brand cereal, how am I supposed to afford another car?

I was talking to my grandpa about the car accident a couple days after, and just so you know… my grandpa has read the Bible dozens of times (no really, I'm not exaggerating). He constantly likes to remind me of the book of Job. It's a tragic story about a man who loses literally every single person and thing he loves; however, throughout all his loss and suffering he never, ever asks God why. All his "friends" tell him that he's being punished by God and that he shouldn't love God anymore. But Job doesn't budge. He loves God. He trusts God. He doesn't ask why.

"If there be a true way that leads to the Everlasting Kingdom, it is most certainly that of suffering, patiently endured."

–St. Colette

After reminding me about the story of Job, my grandpa goes on to tell me, "Does God make mistakes? No. Does God bring good out of everything? Yes." This is something that's so easy to know in your head, but *nearly* impossible in the moment to be convicted of in your heart.

A car accident with minor injuries is a small annoyance compared to some of the pain I know you've probably experienced recently. Where's the joy in this? Where's the hope? Because that whole "my yoke is easy and my burden light" (Matthew 11:30) bit in the Gospel doesn't feel too truthful.

Despair in the face of suffering *can't* be what God wants for us, so what's the secret here?

The Blessed Mother did not have an easy life. She rode a donkey when she was nine months pregnant! (Most pregnant women I've known complain about being uncomfortable lying in bed; can you try to imagine how much worse the prego-life is on the back of a slow moving animal?) She had to give birth in a stable (when Jesus deserved a five-star resort). Then, when she and Joseph brought baby Jesus to the temple a couple days after He was born, she was dealt a pretty rough hand.

> "Love and sacrifice are closely linked, like the sun and the light. We cannot love without suffering and cannot suffer without love."
>
> —St. Gianna Beretta Molla

I've never had a baby but I've seen plenty of new moms. They're usually all excited and "glowy" (aforementioned discomfort totally forgotten), and they all usually gush about how their baby is just the cutest, most adorable little guy ever (cue projectile vomit from said baby).

Mary probably was saying the same sort of things, showing Baby J off at the temple... "Isn't He cute? He rarely cries. And yes, I'm feeling wonderful."

Enter Simon. He's like my older sister who reached out and smashed a piece of origami paper art as soon as I was done admiring it.

First Simon rejoices over being able to see Jesus whom he knows, through God's grace, is the Savior of the world. Then, (in a lot more words, I'm paraphrasing) he tells Mary, "oh and by the way, your heart is going to be pierced by a sword" (Luke 2:22–38).

What else Simon? Are there zombies waiting outside for us? Did someone vandalize our transportation and break the donkey's leg? Do I have chronic bad breath too?

I mean, seriously, what horrible news! What do you do with that kind of bomb dropped on you? If someone came up to you and told you, "you're going to experience great pain in your heart during your life but... we're not going to tell you what or when, so have fun with that storm cloud hanging over your head." Wouldn't you just cry? For days? I would spend every day not enjoying life because I'd be constantly wondering, waiting, and tiptoeing around.

However, Mary accepted this pain as part of her life. Signing up for the job of "God's Mom" wasn't easy and I'm sure she knew that from the moment she uttered her "fiat," her "yes," to participating in God's plan of salvation by being the Mother of God.

Signing up as His disciple isn't easy either. When we make the choice to be followers of Jesus, we're saying "yes" to God's plan for our personal salvation — how He's going to make us saints. He wants to purify us and purification comes through trials and suffering. I'm pretty attached to a lot of worldly comforts. Suffering is God's way of detaching my heart from those lesser things in order to make more room for Him. More God is always better than more mac and cheese.

The culmination of Jesus' mission on earth was also the culmination of the pain in Mary's heart. She watched her beloved Son be beaten until He was nearly dead. She saw Him mocked while a crown of thorns was pressed onto His head — the head she so often kissed goodnight. She was helpless as He carried the cross to Calvary.

Her heart was not only pierced, but slashed and ripped apart as He hung lifeless on the cross. Who of us hasn't felt that kind of pain deep down inside? It's crippling when your parents fight or when you lose a loved one tragically. No one is immune from it. Our world is racked with pain and suffering.

The reason there is so much suffering is because of the sin in the world. It's not a punishment for sin, but a result of living in a fallen world. You see, God didn't have to create the world. He didn't have to create men and women. He did it simply because He wanted to love us and to share heaven with us. He wanted us to love Him back so He created us with the ability to choose whether or not we wanted to love Him. Forced love isn't love at all, which is why God gave us free will.

If we can freely choose to love God, we can also freely choose not to love Him. We're free to choose between forgiveness or anger, charity or gossip, love or hate. No matter how much God wants us to be happy, He doesn't want to control us. The enemy, Satan, has the opportunity to cause a lot of evil in the world through the sin of humans, and since God isn't going to step in and turn us into robots, He doesn't intervene and stop it. That would mean taking away our own and other people's free will to choose between sin and virtue.

See the dilemma here?

But it's not hopeless! God has a really beautiful answer to the problem of pain and suffering. Instead of jumping in and interfering with our free will, He jumped into the human condition and became man so that He could experience everything that we go through.

His answer to pain is the cross. God turned the tables upside down and instead of pain and suffering being the worst thing for men and women, He made it the best thing. Jesus could have saved us any way He wanted. He could have snapped His Godly fingers, or shed a couple drops of blood and opened the gates of heaven. He chose the worst possible death and He did so for one reason: to be more relatable to you and me.

"Nothing great is ever achieved without much enduring."

-St. Catherine of Siena

When you cry, God understands. When you experience excruciating pain, He's been there too. When you're abused, beaten down, dejected, and worn, He knows exactly what that feels like. All you have to do is look at the crucifix to see what God did about your pain. He stepped into our lives to understand it and be with us when we're hurting.

But that's not all; He redeemed it. He didn't just come to experience our pain and suffering — He redeemed it. The cross had a purpose... it led to the Resurrection. Our suffering has a purpose; it's not pointless. When Christ died on the cross as the ultimate sacrifice to save us, He transformed the meaning of suffering from pointless to incredible. Since His death was what won for us grace and salvation, any pain we endure we can give to God to be united to Christ's sacrifice, and He lets us share in the offering and in the grace.

It's a really lofty, theological truth that can be boiled down to this: your pain plus Jesus' suffering, equals special graces for you and your prayer intentions.

I was really blessed that God allowed me to understand the power of prayer and sacrifice first hand. When I was in college my little sister roped me into signing up for an exercise class really early in the morning a couple days a week. I mistakenly thought it was a one day deal and only signed up for the free t-shirt.

Silly me. *Six weeks* later, after I had been getting up at 6:00 am to run, lift, and pushup my way to nausea a couple days a week, I got the free t-shirt. Every day when we went into the gym we were reminded to offer up the workout for a prayer intention (Catholic university, what do you expect?).

Weighing heavily on my heart was a couple I knew who were having a rough time conceiving. They had been trying to have a baby for years and their hearts were broken that they kept miscarrying. I made up my mind to offer up every workout for them. When I didn't want to crunch another ab, or run another lap, or squat another 100 pounds, I said in my mind, "this is for blank and blank" (with blank replaced by their names obviously) and pushed through, offering up the pain for them.

The six week class ended right before Christmas and when I went home for the holidays, I found out that this couple was expecting a baby. They were six weeks pregnant. I had to leave the room to shed some tears of amazement and gratitude that God heard my cries of muscle anguish. I know that He used the graces from my suffering to bless that couple.

You're not alone in your pain, and your pain isn't pointless. Lastly, your pain makes you holier.

Our souls cry out for God, but our bodies cry out for comfort. I think you know which one wins more often. I have a friend who accidentally ordered a double cheeseburger on Good Friday. The wants and needs of our bodies often take priority over our soul because the soul isn't as loud in its demands, and as fallen and sinful humans, we follow in Adam and Eve's footsteps and pick the apple over obedience, food over God, comfort over virtue.

Mary did exactly the opposite of the first woman, Eve. Mary chose God in every instance of hardship. Eve chose to rebel against God when faced with hardship. You and I have that choice too. I don't think we would run away from pain if we realized how it makes us the most like Jesus. C. S. Lewis once said that "pain insists upon being attended to. God whispers to us in our pleasures, speaks in our consciences, but shouts in our pains. It is His megaphone to rouse a deaf world" (*The Problem of Pain*).

In Romans, chapter 6, St. Paul talks about how suffering can lead to new life:

> *"Or are you unaware that we who were baptized into Christ Jesus were baptized into His death? We were indeed buried with Him through baptism into death, so that, just as Christ was raised from the dead by the glory of the Father, we too might live in newness of life" (Romans 6: 3-4).*

The cross is something to be embraced because it's part of who we are as Christians. When Mary stood at the foot of the cross, she taught us that pain isn't something to run from. That doesn't mean you should seek out pain (that's a little weird). But it does mean that when life's circumstances are such that you encounter pain and suffering, you don't have to reject it with every ounce of your being.

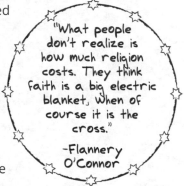

"What people don't realize is how much religion costs. They think faith is a big electric blanket, when of course it is the cross."

-Flannery O'Connor

Mary was able to stand at the cross through unbelievable pain and not run away, or cry out in protest because she honestly believed that God had a plan and was going to make good come from even that horrible situation. Do you believe that? Do you believe that God is all good and that He doesn't lie to us? He said that "whomever follows Me must take up his cross daily" (Luke 9:23), but He also said that He would be close to those who were hurting (Psalm 34:19), that He would make their burden easier (Matthew 11:28), and that through pain, we would be tested and made stronger in our faith (Sirach 2:5).

None of these things make pain and suffering any easier. But they give it perspective. In our greatest moments of suffering, we can experience the greatest amount of grace. If we're open to it, these can also be the moments when we learn and grow the most, and when we take one step closer to sainthood.

Invite God into your suffering. Be open to His grace within your weakest moments. He wants you to learn from your cross, not to waste it. I believe in God because He can make beautiful things come from what appears to be the most terrible circumstances. Only an all-powerful, all-loving God could do that.

It happened with the cross and it can happen in your life too. Try to let go and trust that God is going to work through whatever your burdens are. I know all too well how difficult it is to trust, but I also know it's worth it.

Trust:

Everything is Yours

My ability to trust people has died a tragic death... multiple times. I've had three "best friends" and none of them are a part of my life anymore. I don't care who you are, that's tragic. I know I'm not just being dramatic. (Should I be worried about how proud I am that those two sentences just rhymed?)

It's a scary thing to trust another person with your heart. C.S. Lewis said, "to love at all is to be vulnerable" (*The Four Loves*). That's what happens when you become friends with someone, you share your heart with them and that takes vulnerability. You trust that they won't do things like backstab you, tell your secrets, break their promises, or leave you in the dust like the cartoon *Roadrunner*.

When you give your heart to someone in a dating relationship, there is always the possibility of heartbreak. It can be easy to almost expect it, waiting for something to go wrong before you break up. It can be like holding your breath, waiting to find out how you're not compatible, or that when the sparks fade away and you see clearer, you actually don't really love this person. It's only that one time that you're surprised by someone who doesn't break up with you but instead proposes.

However, with friends, you don't expect to have such heartbreak. There are no sparks igniting and fading away. You don't have to be "compatible" or never annoyed with each other. Friends are supposed to be understanding. You think you're "one soul living in two bodies" and "best friends forever" (Insert sarcastic eye roll).

After I was hurt by my first two best friends, I was *positive* that it wasn't going to happen to me again. I wasn't going to be so careless with my heart and the BFF bracelets. I was going to be really cautious and make sure that anyone else who wanted to be my friend was worth the effort and wasn't someone who would hurt me later.

But how can you be sure? You can't. I lived in a lot of fear with that "what if" constantly hanging over my head and tugging at my heart.

What if this person decides my friendship isn't worth it? What if something tragic happens and I lose them? What if I have really bad body odor and never knew it? What if I have to move to Iceland and can't communicate with anyone? (I like to think I have a healthy imagination.)

Last year my worst fear came true. You know those moments you look back on and wish you could warn yourself about the impending disaster? You look back and wish you could see if there was something, anything you could have changed to make the outcome different. Those are the moments that split your life into a "before" and "after."

I thought my life was awesome. I thought I had myself protected from hurt on all sides. I was safe. I was invincible. I was the Hulk. (Okay, I got carried away. Forget I said that.)

So I was sitting in my office at work, editing a podcast or writing an email or something and I got a text message from my best friend. I could tell you the whole long story but in order to cut out six-eighths of the drama, the grand finale is that in the end she decided we shouldn't be friends anymore and I knew I couldn't fight it; I had to respect her decision.

Tears welled up in my eyes like a scene that belongs in a sappy movie from the 90's — preferably with Mary Kate and Ashley Olsen. I booked it out to my car. I remember driving down the sunny, tree lined street (which is rather obnoxious when you're so upset... sunny skies and trees are great when you're happy, but come on, why the perfect landscaping when I'm sad too?) sobbing and yelling at God through my gasps and waterfall of snot, "What's going on? Why is this happening? FIX IT. And can you please make the skies storm for dramatic effect as well?"

I was shocked. I was miserable. I cried until I felt numb. And then I went back to work because what else do you do when you feel like your life is falling apart? Sometimes routine tasks are comforting during the pain.

Three is a super cool number in the Bible but not so much in my life. Besides the three pets I lost to tragic deaths, I also now lost three BFFs. Not cool, huh?

Do you know what that did to my trust in God? Does "shattered it" paint a clear enough picture? Or maybe "exploded it into smithereens"? My trust in God was about as existent as the T-Rex that lives in my neighborhood.

I felt so betrayed by Him. I should have been looking inward and blaming my poor character judgment, or my tendency to act quite similar to a doormat, or I should have rationally resigned to the reality that we're all broken and imperfect people who make mistakes. Instead, I wrongly chose to blame God.

Not so rational. I was like a little child sitting on my father's lap pounding his chest with my little, harmless fists... for months. "It's all Your fault!" I yelled at Him from the corner of the Adoration chapel, or curled up in the corner of my bed. Like a loving father, not phased by my fits of rage, God just smiles.

When things like this happen, I'm only looking at the current event and feeling in the moment how much it hurts. God, on the other hand, sees the whole picture. I think that's one of the secrets of trust. I think that's what Mary understood too.

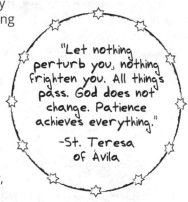

"Let nothing perturb you, nothing frighten you. All things pass. God does not change. Patience achieves everything."

-St. Teresa of Ávila

I was thinking about after Jesus had died and He was taken off the cross by Joseph of Arimathea (Matthew 27:57-60), placed in the arms of Mary, and then laid in the tomb. What was going through Mary's mind?

If I experienced events with that caliber of "tragic," I'm pretty sure I would either want the earth to just swallow me right up, or I would want to hibernate in my bed, under my covers, with a steady supply of delivery pizza and chick-flicks so I could numb myself and not think about the horror of what just happened. My reaction to tragic events is totally inward focused. I can't believe this happened to me. What am I going to do? I hurt. I feel hopeless. Help *me*.

Mary held His dead body as it came off the cross. She felt the lack of life, the quiet stillness instead of the rise and fall of His chest as He breathed. He was gone. Her only son, her beloved Jesus was dead.

According to what she could see in front of her.

Everything pointed to Jesus' destruction. She saw His life expire and the proof was lying in her arms. What was the point anymore? Did she wonder "what now?" Did she ask herself what was the point of all the miracles and ministry, of all the preaching and prayer?

No matter whether or not she was let in on the secret of His eventual victory over death, don't you think she would've wondered if the plan didn't work? Or what went wrong?

Maybe she did wonder those things but one thing's for sure, she didn't make a scene about it. I think that would've made it into the Gospel... "And then the woman, His mother, was hysterical and unresponsive, overcome with shock and emotion."

Everyone would have understood if she fell into despair. She would've had every right to react in whatever way she wanted. That was her only son. They had spent 33 years together, making memories and growing in their relationship.

That was my best friend. We had spent a couple years together, making memories and growing in our relationship.

But those things don't matter when God has a better plan. You can say, "Jesus I trust in You" a million times but if that trust isn't put to the test they're just empty words. This is a pretty basic principle, right? If you say you love someone but don't show them your love, they're not going to believe you.

If everything in our lives, including relationships, are gifts from God, then who are we to feel this sense of entitlement? We don't deserve anything He's given us out of generosity. We can't say, "this is mine, how dare you ruin it?"

There's a song I love by Audrey Assad and the lyrics go, "If everything is Yours I'm letting it go. It was never mine to hold."

That's what I would call *radical* trust.

Mary had this kind of trust. Jesus was always the Son of God first. He was both God and man. He wasn't hers to hold in the first place so she offered Him back to God at the end of His life. And she offers Him to us. His life was for our sake. His death was for our sake. Her pain was for our sake.

No matter what she felt inside, or how she wanted to react, her trust in God was stronger. She lived out Proverbs 3:5-6, "Trust in the Lord with all your heart and lean not on your own understanding."

Christ never guaranteed an easy life and the sin of this world ensures that. He promised the cross to the faithful, but He also promised His help: "Take up your cross and learn from Me for My yoke is easy and My burden light" (Luke 9:23).

> "Totally love Him, who gave Himself totally for your love."
> —St. Clare

Notice how He didn't say that there is no burden. There's always a burden; we live in a fallen world. Hate to break it you.

Mary felt that burden. I have felt that burden so often. I know you have too. You know what this feels like. You know what heartbreak is, what pain feels like. You can identify with that desire to lash out in anger at God, to turn your back on Him because life didn't go according to your plan and now you want to curl up in a ball and eat brownies.

Who is God though if we can't trust Him? He is perfect, which means He is completely worthy of our trust. No matter how many of my life circumstances should point to chaos, they don't. In faith, I see that God can bring good out of anything. Yes, my heart has been wounded, but it's in those times of pain and darkness that I look at that image of Mary holding her Son and throw myself into her arms too, right there along with Jesus.

When I felt like I couldn't trust God, I never gave up pounding on God's chest until I got the result I wanted. Little kids can be annoying like that; however, my rant changed over time from "why?" and "how could You?" to "show me Your way," and "help me understand."

Slowly, so...very...slowly, I grew in my trust and was able to let go of the anger. It's not like you wake up one day, jump out of bed, and run around yelling, "I see the light! I understand! I'm not sad anymore!"

I mean, Mary was pretty lucky because she only spent three days praying and wondering what was going to happen. Then Jesus rose from the dead and I can just imagine her with this little smile on her face as she said to Him, "I knew it was going to be okay."

What if we echoed that every day? I know it's going to be okay God. I know it's going to be okay. It might take time. I know it's going to hurt, but I trust You. I know it's going to be okay.

"The more lofty the degree of loving union to which God destines the soul, so much more profound and persistent must be its purification."

-St. Teresa Benedicta of the Cross

He has a plan that's way bigger than anything we can imagine. We see what's in front of our eyes but He sees the mountaintop view, the whole tapestry of our lives. Doesn't that mean He deserves our trust?

Think about it: Didn't God conquer death and rise from the grave? Didn't He rescue you from sin and open heaven for you? Didn't God wake you up again today? Didn't He give us chocolate?

He wants what's best for you, even if that means breaking your heart in the process of getting there. My heart still hurts over the friendship that I lost, but I had to make a choice to forgive her, even in the midst of the pain. Although we aren't friends anymore, I'm still able to remember some of the good times from our friendship.

One of the things that I remember fondly from our friendship is that her and I had this saying that we would remind each other of when one of us was going through something difficult. We would say: "Hard is not bad... hard is just hard."

Trust means that you don't run away from pain and heartbreak when life gets hard. It means you embrace it, knowing that just because it's difficult, doesn't mean it's permanent or pointless. God has a plan that's bigger and better, and that plan will make you a saint. I have to remind myself of this all the time... daily, hourly, and even every five minutes on a bad day. That's okay though because it means I'm trying.

I'm learning more and more what true friendship means and what a healthy relationship is. Mary's example taught me that temporary suffering is worth the eternal prize of happiness in heaven. Eternal happiness in heaven is always God's plan for us, and God will use everything that happens in our lives to help us get there.

Modern Feminism:

Girls Rule, Boys Drool

I grew up watching my dad open doors for my mom and seeing him teach my brother to do the same. It was called "being a gentleman" and it was something that was not only courteous but expected of the men in my family. "Ladies before gentlemen" was a phrase that meant we got first dibs on gram's fried chicken at family get-togethers.

Seemed like a cool idea to me.

I didn't know I was supposed to take offense when guys gave women this special treatment. At least not until college. That's when I met Jen.

Jen was loud, proud, and the life of the crowd. Everyone loved her and when she gave her opinion on something it was spoken with such confidence and vehemence that if you wanted to disagree you better have a very good counter-argument.

She said that because women were equal to men it was offensive to be treated differently from a man. To be given any kind of special treatment (especially from a man) was annoying.

Jen said, "When a guy holds open a door, it's like he's implying that I'm not capable of taking care of myself. And that's offensive to me!"

And I said, "oh..."

But then I thought about it for roughly about 13 months. Sometimes it takes me a long time to process things. (You should see me trying to pick out an outfit to wear!) Every time a guy would hold a door open, or offer to carry something for me, or let me go ahead of him — I felt uncomfortable.

I didn't know what to think. I didn't want to be treated as lower than a man, but I also wasn't so sure that's what they meant when they held open a door. Did that kind, muscular man think he had to take care of me? I'm an adult! I thought. I'm in college and I know how to check the oil in my car. I just won a flag football game... I sure as heck don't need someone to open a door for me!

I slowly became angry when guys would act chivalrous. Me along with every other misguided feminist out there. If feminism is about equality, then one gender doing things for the other isn't right. If men really understood our dignity, we wouldn't be treated differently. We wouldn't be expected to dress up and wear heels and be dainty.

One half of the feminist agenda is that it's crippling to a woman's freedom and we need to be liberated from the idea that women should to be *confined* only to traditional gender roles. We need to free ourselves from the image of the perfectly shaped woman, wearing a dress and heels and standing in front of the stove with a couple happy children at her feet. That's not the only thing women are good for. The kitchen or bedroom isn't the only place we have worth.

"Each woman who lives in the light of eternity can fulfill her vocation, no matter if it is in marriage, in a religious order, or in a worldly profession."

-St. Teresa Benedicta of the Cross

That's the message of feminism I can get behind. I don't want to feel guilty for wearing jeans and Toms on some days... or for pursuing a career in something I love instead of waiting around for a man to produce children with.

However, the other half of the modern feminist movement says that this idea of "gender equality" means that there's no *difference* between the genders. Man, woman... same thing... in all places and situations except bed.

I feel weird about that. I can't check the box of approval on that idea. Men and women *are* very different.

If we were the same at our core, why did God make both Adam and Eve? Why not just make one gender? That definitely would've saved some time and Adam a rib. God made us male and female because *both* are necessary. Neither sex "has it all" and we are made to be complementary to each other. It's frustrating though because the things that we as women lack and men have are looked at as our weaknesses.

You can look at our sensitive hearts as being a weakness because feeling things deeply can leave us crying pretty often. While this is great for tissue companies, a lot of men (and some women) see that as a flaw. Women also have a certain way of looking at situations, seeing things as more person centered rather than fact-centered like men. These are seen as weaknesses because somewhere along the line it was decided that strength and accomplishments were the ideal and that being sensitive is a sign of being inferior.

The modern feminist movement, though often misguided, can't be fully blamed for wanting to elevate and "free" women because we've been put down and labeled as the weaker, lesser gender for longer than you can remember. Pope John Paul II said,

> "When it comes to setting women free from every kind of exploitation and domination, the Gospel contains an ever relevant message which goes back to the attitude of Jesus Christ Himself. Transcending the established norms of His own culture, Jesus treated women with openness, respect, acceptance and tenderness. In this way He honored the dignity which women have always possessed according to God's plan and in His love" (Pope John Paul II, Letter to Women).

Jesus was radical in how He treated women. The women that were followers of Jesus were allowed to walk around with the men, and Jesus didn't treat them as the "lesser" beings that everyone else saw them as. These women were accustomed to being made to feel inferior, to being used, and told they weren't worthy of education, only childbearing. Jesus taught by His example and held them in high esteem just like the male apostles. Read John 8:1-11; it's the story of the woman who was caught in sin and she's about to be stoned by a crowd of people.

Notice how she was caught "in the act of adultery" but the man got away without any condemnation? The woman was to blame.

The crowd asks Jesus what they should do and He tells them that the person who has never sinned should throw the first stone. When they slowly walk away, He looks up at the woman with mercy and love and tells her that He's not going to condemn her either... when He had every right to. You'd think that justice requires adequate punishment according to the sin; however, Jesus' love and mercy is the card that trumps everything else. He treated her with the dignity she deserved, regardless of her past mistakes, regardless of her weaknesses, regardless that she fell into the sin of adultery.

> "I will go anywhere and do anything in order to communicate the love of Jesus to those who do not know Him or have forgotten Him."
>
> -St. Frances Xavier Cabrini

The women who were Jesus' disciples followed Him because they were treasured and treated with the dignity that they deserved. The women at the foot of the cross were further breaking social barriers. They weren't content to sit at home crying, or stay in the background of the story. Fierce attachment to Jesus born from an encounter with Him is what inspired these women to be bold in their femininity. They had sensitive hearts, so instead of staying home weeping, they went to the tomb.

Mary, who obviously is a woman, is the one human person who God made the most glorified, exulted, and esteemed... like ever.

> *"It is in the New Testament that the full glory of the female mission and vocation shines in the person of the Holy Virgin of Nazareth"* (Alice Von Hildebrand, The Privilege of Being a Woman).

God chose a woman as His vehicle into this world. Do you get how incredibly amazing that is? I think it deserves to be repeated... Jesus came into our world by becoming smaller than your pinky fingernail and He made a home within the womb of a woman for nine months. God is bigger and better than you can imagine Him, and yet He became smaller and more vulnerable than you can imagine Him. He put Himself totally in the care of a woman, the creature He made and valued so highly.

When God chose to come into this world through a woman, our whole gender was instantly elevated. Our identity and vocation and mission were all revealed in that moment. Edith Stein, also known as St. Teresa Benedicta of the Cross, said that:

> *"Only the person blinded by the passion of controversy could deny that woman in soul and body is formed for a particular purpose. The clear and irrevocable world of Scripture declares what daily experience teaches from the beginning of the world: woman is destined to be wife and mother"* (The Ethos of Woman's Professions).

When I was in college I took a class in "embryology" which is the study of an embryo, a baby, from conception to birth. It was fascinating and I was enthralled by what a beautifully intricate and well thought-out process a baby goes through during that first part of their life. I learned something in that class that blew my mind when I applied it to Mary pregnant with Jesus.

After the miraculous events of the Incarnation, Jesus was knit in Mary's womb just like any other human baby is. That means that Mary's body was the one that gave Jesus His. Her blood flowed through His veins. Awesome right? Well here's the amazing part. Did you know that every mother, based on the simple fact that she carries the baby for nine months, ends up with some of that baby's cells in her own body. That means my mom still has some cells from each of her six kids in her body. Even after Mary gave birth to Jesus, she still had cells that were Jesus' inside of her! How mind blowing is that?![1]

But wait! There's more! You can have Jesus in you too and it doesn't require you to carry Jesus in your womb. When you receive the Eucharist, you are literally taking Jesus' body, blood, soul, and divinity into your blood stream. God is pumping through your veins. This is a central teaching of Catholicism, that during the consecration, although the bread and wine don't change in appearance to your senses, the substance of the bread and wine changes, unseen to the eye, and it is really and truly the body, blood, soul, and divinity of Christ. This is the truth even though it still looks and tastes like bread and wine. If you've received communion, you are walking around with God's very BEING inside of you.

---

[1] Dawe, G., Tan, X. W., & Xiao, Z. (n.d.). Cell Migration from Baby to Mother. National Center for Biotechnology Information. Retrieved August 1, 2013, from www.ncbi.nlm.nih.gov/pmc/articles/PMC26

There's one more thing. And this just brought tears to my eyes. (Because yes, I'm a woman and I feel things very deeply and I'm owning that right now!) When the cells of the baby migrate to the mother, they can stay there for decades. Do you know what these particular cells do? **They have the tendency to target sites of injury and aid in healing.**

Think about that. The cells of Jesus that were inside Mary helped in any physical injury she experienced in her body. But let's take it to the spiritual level. God is a healer of our wounds and He wants to be as close to us as possible. So, He reduces Himself to the form of bread because we wouldn't be able to handle His unbridled glory. Moses couldn't look at Him, how would we be able to consume Him if He didn't hide all His glory within the bread and wine? Once inside our blood stream, He targets our wounds. He heals us from the inside out.

The wounds we have of being put down as the "weaker sex" or of being objectified and made to feel like we're only good for our bodies and any pleasure we can give a man — God wants to heal that hurt. When you feel like you need to prove yourself by becoming more masculine, and apologizing for your femininity, God comes to heal you and show you how lovable you are, just as you are.

I believe that the Eucharist is the antidote to the disconnect between men and women. God doesn't discriminate. He doesn't pick sides. He doesn't say that He loves one of us more than the other. He is the great equalizer among us. He's the common denominator. You'd think if one sex was better than the other, God would give the better gender more privileges. Nope.

"The soul cannot live without love. She always wants to love something because love is the stuff she is made of."

-St. Catherine of Siena

Both men and women can use who God made them to be as a motivator to grow closer to Him. It's a woman's weaknesses that (ideally) are her strengths because it motivates her to rely more on God for everything. Likewise, you could say a man's physical and emotional strength are what can lead him to turn to God to learn humility and gentleness.

We don't need to be at odds with one another. There doesn't have to be a competition. I think Jen, my friend in college, was wrong in feeling threatened by a man's chivalry, his acts of kindness as a gentleman towards a woman. Men and women can appreciate each other for their differences without feeling inadequate and belittled for the way that God intentionally made us.

When a man is a gentleman towards you, it's a compliment. It's an affirmation of everything good in you. It's a man saying that he doesn't want anything from you. In this instance you don't have to worry about being objectified. Chivalry isn't about how good you look; it's about your dignity as a woman.

I think that true feminism is living into the things that make you a woman and being confident in your femininity while being equipped with God's truth that you are made to be fully alive and fully you.

An authentic feminist who is a strong, faithful woman doesn't have to negate chivalry but can appreciate chivalry for its pure motives. We can let men treat us with the dignity that we deserve when everyone else is reducing us to simply a sexual object. If feminism is about women being freed from the idea that we're only good for babies and baking, isn't that exactly what chivalry is affirming? You have worth because you're a beautiful daughter of God, not for some other shallow reason.

One thing that isn't helping the world to stop seeing us in a shallow way is immodesty. If you bare it all you're sending the message that your body is the best thing about you. We have to stand up for our worth as women by demanding to be seen as more than a collection of body parts. It starts with you.

The world needs girls who are so excited to be girls. Being "that one girl" that makes an impact on this world doesn't mean being only one kind of girl. You can do whatever you want with your life; being a woman doesn't have to limit you. Instead, you can use your femininity to enhance everything you do! Edith Stein said, "Every profession in which woman's soul comes into its own and which can be formed by woman's soul is an authentic woman's profession" (*The Ethos of Woman's Professions*).

The world needs women to enhance different professions, but the world also needs women who will embrace their call to be amazing mothers and raise children who will change the world.

We also need women who will be spiritual mothers to whomever they encounter. The world needs us to use our feminine heart to bring more love and compassion into this often cruel world. The world already has men that are doing a pretty great job of being all puffed up about being men. It's our turn. We have so much to offer from our femininity. Pope John Paul II called our unique heart, sensitivities, and way of seeing the world as the "feminine genius." If that doesn't make you feel awesome go take a nap and come back and read it again. I wish I could get all the modern feminists in a room and simply tell them, "stop trying to be like men when you were made with so many special characteristics as a woman. It's okay to be different because different doesn't mean lesser."

Lastly, I just have to add: Do realize you can instantly one-up any man at any time, right? When he's telling you about how he can build blah, blah, blah... and what an impressive car he has, blah, blah, blah...

"My body can hold a life inside it." Boom.

You are an incredible and intricate work of art and we're part of a Church that's passionate about appreciating you as a woman. And if you ever feel put down, degraded, or objectified for your femininity, get to Mass and receive the Eucharist. Ask God to heal those wounds and then run to Mary and ask her to pray with you and for you.

Rosary:
Carry Me Mama

I started disliking the rosary from the time I was old enough to like and dislike things. Our family prayed the rosary every single night after dinner. It took away from more Barbie playtime; therefore, it wasn't fun. It was a time to sit close to my siblings and annoy each other with pokes, glares, and mean faces. Sometimes it was just a time to sleep. At any rate, it was not my favorite time.

Then, when I was a junior in high school, I fell in love with my faith and with being Catholic. I met a couple of young adults who modeled for me what a joy it was to be Catholic and how to simultaneously be cool and be on fire for God. After that, I began praying the rosary willingly on my own. So, I prayed it by myself.

"You pay God a compliment by asking great things of Him."

-St. Teresa of Avila

For an entire summer I never missed a day. It helped that it didn't take very long because I'm a speed pray-er.

This discipline forced me to focus my day on God, and giving Mary all the intentions that were on my heart brought me an incredible sense of peace knowing that she, my mother, was going to take care of it all.

Giving Mary your prayer intentions is like handing her some raw meat. She takes it, seasons it, cooks it up, makes a couple colorful side dishes for presentation, and brings it to Jesus all tasty and aromatic and worthy of winning a Chef's reality show. This is something that's super important to understand about our Catholic faith — we don't pray "to" Mary, we pray *with* her and ask her to pray for us.

"There is no problem, I tell you, no matter how difficult it is, that we cannot solve by the prayer of the Holy Rosary."

-Sister Lucia of Fatima

Jesus doesn't really like to say "no" to His mom. Wedding at Cana anyone (John 2:1-11)? Jesus and Mary were at a wedding and He was not about to start His public ministry, but He didn't want to say no when Mary asked Him to work His first public miracle — changing water into wine. I wonder if it's the eyes. Did she pull a sad, puppy face on Him? Does Mary have a certain voice that you can't quite say no to? No, she wouldn't need to do that. He just loves her so much that He wants to do what she asks.

Having Mary on your side is like having your own personal cheerleader and life coach. She advocates for us before God's throne, and she offers wisdom from the example of her life through the mysteries of the rosary. The words repeated over and over are just the soundtrack behind your meditation on the events of Jesus and Mary's life.

Pope Paul VI said:

> *"Without contemplation, the rosary is a body without a soul, and its recitation runs the risk of becoming a mechanical repetition of formulas [...] By its nature the recitation of the rosary calls for a quiet rhythm and a lingering pace, helping the individual to meditate on the mysteries of the Lord's life as seen through the eyes of her who was closest to the Lord. In this way the unfathomable riches of these mysteries are disclosed"* (Apostolic Exhortation Marialis Cultus).

I love to pray about each virtue that has been assigned to each mystery. If you've never heard of this or prayed with them, look it up the next time you go to pray. Instead of just thinking about the Annunciation, you meditate on Mary's humility in that situation. For the Visitation, we think about Mary's "love of neighbor" and ask for an increase in our own. I love praying about the virtue of poverty that goes along with the mystery for the birth of Christ.

It breaks up the monotony of the rosary. I think that's why I couldn't stand praying the rosary as a child — I thought it was so boring. But it wasn't the rosary that was boring, it was me.

> *"When lovers are together, they spend hours and hours repeating the same thing: I love you! What is missing in the people who think the Rosary monotonous, is Love" (Sr. Lucia of Fatima).*

I was missing love - love for Mary and love for my faith. As I began to pray the rosary more purposefully, my love for Christ and His mother grew.

To pray the rosary is to be held within Mary's embrace.

When I was in high school I was a nanny for my little cousins. My aunt and uncle have four adorable girls and when I started watching them the youngest, Natalie, was only two years old. Most kids fuss and cry over naptime, but at 1:00 pm every day, Natalie was more than willing to head upstairs to read books and take a nap. But she had to do it herself. It didn't matter that the long staircase was ominously looming over her, or that she had to climb it on all fours. She did not want my help getting up the stairs.

The first couple steps were conquered with much vigor, but I could tell the next two were a bit difficult to her. That lunch coma was starting to set in, and running around the house really wears a kid out (especially when you have such a fun nanny). By the time she had only gotten about five steps up, she would just stop and lie there, sprawled vertically on the stairs.

"Do you want me to carry you now?" No answer was necessary as she reached up for me, blanket in one hand. At first she was alert in my arms, but by the time we reached the top she was resting on my shoulder, sucking her thumb and practically asleep. As much as she thought she could, she wasn't able to make it upstairs herself.

Some of my favorite images of Mary are of her holding baby Jesus, especially when He is peacefully asleep in her arms. I love to put myself in the picture and imagine myself as that infant. I've often found comfort in being that baby resting against Mary's heart. There's nothing to worry about when you're safe in her embrace.

Mary sees all of our anxieties and exhaustion, and she says, "Do you want me to carry you?" If you don't reach up for her, if you don't pick up those rosary beads, you're not giving her the opportunity to carry you to Jesus. We can't do it ourselves and we weren't meant to. Running around this life is tiring; Mary wants to carry you up to Jesus so that He can refresh you. Don't be too stubborn to reach out to her.

> *"Some people are so foolish that they think they can go through life without the help of the Blessed Mother. Love the Madonna and pray the rosary, for her rosary is the weapon against the evils of the world today. All graces given by God pass through the Blessed Mother" (St. Padre Pio).*

Assumption and Coronation:

How to Win at Life

Here's the thing. In the end, Mary won at life... she is now in heaven!

She chose God every single day, she reached the height of virtue, and she fully allowed God to work in her life. Christ's victory over sin and death allowed her to live a life "full of grace."

When her time here on this earth was over, she was assumed into heaven, body and soul. As she took her last breathe on earth that was also her first moment in heaven. God couldn't let her sacred, sinless body experience any decay so both her body and her soul went right to heaven. I bet she left some very bewildered people back on earth.

I like to imagine Mary entering heaven to the epic scene of rejoicing angels and saints. Think of the biggest football stadium you can... filled with people all cheering excitedly... now multiply that by the biggest number you can think of and I feel like that's a tiny sliver of what it was like when she entered heaven.

Then, to top it all off (literally... pun very much intended), she is crowned as the Queen of Heaven. Didn't see that one coming did ya' Mary? All the holiest people I know are also the most humble people I know. I don't think Mary would have thought she was going to be made Queen of Heaven. She perfected all the virtues — that includes humility. She was just happy to have been able to be an instrument of God and participate in His saving plan. I'm sure she would have been very happy leaving it at that.

But God didn't just leave it at that. This woman hadn't just helped Him out with His plan of salvation, she was majorly important. She was necessary for Him to be able to save us from sin. Not to mention, she is the spouse of the Holy Spirit and God wouldn't simply give her an ordinary (albeit beautiful) place in heaven alongside countless holy souls.

God wanted to honor Mary. And, boy, was she honored. I can just imagine her being like, "Me? Really? Wow... I just love you all so much... I'd like to thank my Mom and Dad... and Joseph for being so supportive... " or something along those lines. Jesus took the commandment to love thy father and mother to a whole new level.

"Be who God meant you to be and you will set the world on fire."

-St. Catherine of Siena

She won at life. She chose to love and serve God every moment of every day, even when the world was coming at her from all sides. It wasn't easy for her either; life wasn't a stroll down the beach. Don't make the mistake of doubting that she deserves her title and her honors.

So what does that mean for us? Why does it matter that she was assumed into heaven and now reigns as Queen there? So what?

It means a lot. And all because I'm still struggling; I know you are too. I think you know by now that I haven't got this life all figured out. I'm such a work in progress. You know more about my faults than my little sister and she can sure tell you a lot of my faults. Sometimes I feel like everything is difficult and I can't do anything right and I'll never be virtuous or have a good day.

What's a "good" day anyway? One where you look nice and say nice things, find a great sale at your favorite store, and then have lunch with your best friend? Maybe it's those things, but it also means that you've chosen God and His way and truths in all things. That's a good day.

So what if you have more bad days than good ones? Well, you're still going at it, right? You're still trying to be a holy woman and that's what matters. It doesn't matter how often you mess it up, what matters is that you don't give up. The point is that Mary, our mother, is in a position in heaven to always be there for you, whether you call upon her or not. Moms never stop caring about their children.

One day two of my friends from work and I decided to go inner tubing down a river here in Phoenix, Arizona. It's a very popular spot for us desert-dwellers to go and hang out to get a little relief from the heat. Since it was the weekend, the river was very crowded, mostly with rowdy groups of people.

We were just there to relax and enjoy the water and each other's company but it was hard to do surrounded by floating parties of people. This stressed me out from the moment we got there because I had been a lifeguard for the last five years and knew all too well how dangerous the combination of water and alcohol can be. At a couple points on the three hour ride down the water, there were some rapids that took some skill and balance to navigate, but not anything strong enough to majorly freak you out.

As the three of us were being whisked through one such patch of rapids, we passed by a young man yelling at a woman and struggling to hold onto her as the water tried equally as hard to pull her away from him. The man's foul cursing initially made us think he was just angry at the woman, but as we drifted farther away we heard his cries change to pleas for help.

"What should we do? We have to help them!" we said to one another. We immediately began attempting to get to the side of the river, a very difficult task amidst the rushing rapids. Once we got to the side, we were already a couple hundred feet downstream from where the man was standing in the water, holding onto the woman. Running as fast as we could, we headed in their direction and when we were a couple yards away, the man couldn't fight the water anymore. His strength gave out and the woman slipped away from him.

My lifeguard's instinct kicked in and the three of us dashed out into the river, keeping our eyes fixed on her motionless body as she slipped under the water. I lunged toward her and managed to hook my arm under her armpit while simultaneously digging my knees into the rough, rocky, river bottom. Her heavy, limp body, combined with the rushing water was almost more than I could bear. I thought I was going to seriously injure one of my legs, not knowing what rocks or obstructions I was about to be smashed into under the water. I clutched the woman's body and attempted to move sideways over to the shore. Thank goodness I only had to drag her a little ways before my friends were able to help me bring her out of the water.

As it turns out, the young man was her son and she had overdosed on drugs and alcohol while being out in the hot sun on the river. She remained unresponsive for about an hour, then slowly started to return to normal.

We left the river that day incredibly shaken by what had happened. The woman had no recollection of her near-death experience and I'm sure we will never see her again.

It was one of those situations where you're just in the right place at the right time. I can tell you with absolute certainty that there was a lot of Divine assistance going on. I know that from the moment we saw those two people in distress, all three of us prayed for them, whether it was with words or simply in our hearts. I specifically remember sending up to heaven a desperate "help" as I was fighting to grab onto her before she got too far downstream or spent too long underwater.

In those terrifying moments, and in the seconds of strength and victory, it didn't matter that Mary didn't appear in a flash of radiant light, she was present there. She was praying for us, and doing whatever she could to keep us safe. We are never alone in our most challenging moments because our mother in heaven is always looking out for us.

Life can be discouraging — but look up. Life can be exhausting — look up. All around you there are messages (maybe in your own head) telling you that you're not good enough — look up. She's there. She's Queen of heaven and earth. She's up in heaven cheering you on, waiting for you to ask her to pray for you and praying for you even when you don't ask her to. That's what a mom does. Your heavenly mother wants you to get to heaven, and to get to heaven you have to cooperate with God's grace in order to win at life too!

There's nothing to win if there's no battle to fight.

Please, don't be ashamed of your struggles. We've all been there. The worst thing you can do is to pretend those struggles aren't there and to avoid dealing with them. A wise woman once told me, "silence keeps us sick." We need to let it out. Talk about it. Be proactive about pursuing a healthy, holy lifestyle. These things don't just happen while you're watching a movie. If you need to talk with a professional, that's fine! If you have a wise mentor-figure in your life, take advantage of that! Lean on your friends. Lean on your youth minister. But most importantly, lean on the Sacraments.

> "The youth are the future. The young people have only one life and it's worth it to spend it well!"
>
> -Blessed Chiara Luce Badano

I don't want you to be ashamed of your battle because that's what God is using to make you a saint. He's trying to bring you home to Him and that might be the means He's going to use. I don't know if it's perfectionism, body image, trust, purity, relationships, emotions, or all the above plus a few others. Whatever it is, Mary is right there beside you in it all. Our mom rocks. She wants you to know that she doesn't abandon any of her children. When you come to her, she can't not help you in some way. The Memorare, a common prayer, shows us that she always is there to help us:

> Remember oh most gracious Virgin Mary, that **never was it known that anyone who fled to thy protection, implored thy help, or sought thy intercession was left un-aided.** Inspired by this confidence I fly unto you or Virgin of virgins my mother. To thee do I come, before thee I stand, sinful and sorrowful. Oh Mother of the Word Incarnate, despise not my petitions but in thy mercy, hear and answer me. Amen.

She won't let you down. She knows your name and who you have a crush on. Mary just wants to lead you to her Son and her Queenship only reiterates that. She's His right hand, His mama, and she's talking to Him about you. St. Thomas Aquinas once said this about Mary: "As mariners are guided into port by the shining star, so Christians are guided to heaven by Mary."

You win at life when you let God win and you live out who God made you to be. Mary was authentically feminine. She was fully alive and her life was fully a gift to God.

When I screw up, when I do something stupid, or when I need Divine help in my day to day life, I allow God to win in those moments by seeking His mercy and His love. I'm on the rocky road to heaven until I get there. We have to give ourselves permission to be saints in the making. Sometimes winning is all about what you're telling yourself. If you're consistently negative you'll be consistently unhappy.

Winning is also about finding the good in every situation. We have to be girls who live in God's truth, not the world's lies. Ask Him for the grace to know and understand His truths. By embracing the graces He always wants to pour down on us, we can be the kind of woman Mary was.

"You cannot be half a saint; you must be a whole saint or no saint at all."

-St. Thérèse of Lisieux

Let's celebrate each other and celebrate the amazing gift it is to be a woman. It may not feel like an amazing gift to be a woman every 28 days when you're rummaging for chocolate, but it is. Every single one of us is so beautiful and I hope you've heard that before, but if you haven't, I hope you can believe it now. There's no one else like you.

You're that one girl — the only one who can be you. And you know what? As awesome as she was, the world doesn't need another Mary. It needs women who are trying to emulate Mary's virtues. The world needs you right now. God could have placed you in any country, in any town, in any year He wanted. He chose right now for a reason. Don't give up the fight for sainthood and for holy womanhood.

Mary knows what it's like; she knows how you feel. She was a girl just like you and I, she went through the same sorts of struggles, and she let God win. She won so that she could be the mom who shows you how it all works. How sad would it be if we went through life only seeing her as a statue in the corner of the church?

That's it really. That's all I've got. I think of you as my sister and I want you to know that I'm praying for you. I love you even though I don't know you. My only hope is that you get to know that one girl who changed the course of salvation history, so that empowered by a relationship with Mary, you can change the course of history today.

✿ Discussion Questions ✿

Chapter 1: Perfectionism

Has anyone (or even yourself) ever placed unrealistic expectations on you and your behavior and choices? Why do you think they (or you) did that?

In what areas of your life do you feel like you have to be perfect?

What are some examples of people who have failed in some regard but were still successful, holy, and saintly?

Talk about one way that you failed this week. What happened? How was it resolved? What did you learn from it? How can you forgive yourself?

Chapter 2: Body Image

What are the messages you see and hear about what you're supposed to look like?

Why is it easy to believe these messages and let them dictate our thoughts and behaviors?

Do you have any unhealthy attitudes about your body and about food? What can you do to change those attitudes?

Spend some time affirming one another, not only for physical beauty, but for soul beauty too.

How can you bring Christ to the people around you in more concrete ways?

Chapter 3: Purity

Have you ever been judgmental towards someone who struggles with purity? Why?

How has your perception of your dignity and worth been tainted?

What kind of man do you believe you deserve?

What are some good ways to handle temptations? Make a list of the things you can do to avoid temptation.

Chapter 4: Emotions

What is the attitude about emotions in your home? Do you think it's healthy or unhealthy? How has that affected you?

Do you ever experience shame for feeling a lot of emotions? What can you do to accept the fact that God made you with a sensitive heart?

What would it look like if you used your strong emotions for compassion and empathy?

What are some healthy ways that you can express your emotions instead of bottling them up or pouring them all out at once?

Make a list of all the emotions that you most commonly feel. Which emotions do you need to speak truth to and what are those truths?

Chapter 5: Anger

What feelings are you afraid of expressing? And who are you afraid of disappointing if you express that feeling?

When was a time when you suppressed a strong feeling? What was the result?

What are some of the rules in your mind of the things you think you "should" do and feel and how has it made you negative?

How do you deal with anger? What are some positive and non-destructive ways that you can handle anger?

Take some time to create a mental image of a place where you and Jesus can go and sit and just be together.

Chapter 6: Friendship

What other qualities do you think make up a healthy friendship?

What qualities are unhealthy in a friendship?

What are some ways that you can bring Christ to your friends?

What kinds of things do you need to do to take care of yourself that should be a priority in your life?

How can you be sure you're allowing God to fill your heart, instead of trying to fulfill yourself in your relationships?

Chapter 7: Daily Life

What are the most boring, mundane parts of your week?

How would you see those things differently if you invited God into them?

Talk about the needs that you have. Are you meeting those needs?

How can you help yourself fulfill your needs in healthier ways?

Read Romans 12:9-21. Use it as a way to examine your day, your week, your life. How can you live out this advice from St. Paul in a healthy way in your day-to-day life?

Chapter 8: Suffering

What is your initial reaction to pain and suffering? Especially in relation to God?

Can you think of a different response that you'd ideally like to have? How can you turn to God in your pain?

Make a list of the prayer intentions that are heaviest upon your heart and share them with a trusted friend so that the two of you can pray for those intentions.

Chapter 9: Trust

What has caused you to lose a little bit of your trust in God? Have you been honest with God about it?

What are some of the reasons and the evidence that you've seen to prove that God is trustworthy?

What do you need to trust God with right now?

How would your prayer and life change if you weren't worried or fearful but rather, trusting?

Chapter 10: Modern Feminism

How do you feel about men acting like gentlemen towards you? If it makes you uncomfortable why do you think that is?

What do you consider to be your weaknesses as a woman? How can these things lead you closer to God?

What do you love about being a woman and what do you dislike? How can you use your femininity to bring God glory?

Read John 8:1-11 aloud and imagine yourself as the woman in the story. Feel the love and mercy of Christ as He comes into your worst moments and offers you unconditional love and not condemnation for your weaknesses.

Chapter 11: Rosary

How do you feel about praying the rosary?

What situations in your life make you want to give up?

Like Jesus changed the water into wine at Cana, what do you need to entrust to Mary, knowing that God will work miracles if you allow Him to?

What can you give up in order to have more time to pray the rosary?

Take this time to pray the rosary together, or just one decade if you can't pray the whole thing.

Chapter 12: Assumption and Coronation

What negative things do you tell yourself that are holding you back from being the best, happiest person you can be?

What can you do to claim victory over your everyday battles?

How will you continue to grow in your relationship with Mary?

Do you know how beloved and beautiful you are? What do you love about yourself and what are some of your goals for your life?

Share ways that you can continue to be a support to one another and celebrate the gift of femininity with each other.

Full of Grace

A Teen Guide to the Rosary

Make the rosary come alive in your own life with Life Teen's newest pocket-sized book: *Full of Grace: A Teen Guide to the Rosary*. Written for any soul wanting to grow closer to Christ and His mother; *Full of Grace* will not only teach you how to pray the Rosary, but also guide you into a daily prayer routine with the Rosary. As you pray with *Full of Grace*, you'll be drawn into the story of each Mystery of the Rosary through relatable and intimate reflections, perfect for all ages. Transform your prayer life today with *Full of Grace: A Teen Guide to the Rosary*.

This book includes:

- A step-by-step guide to praying the Rosary.

- An interesting and entertaining History of the Rosary.

- Direct Scripture passages associated with each Mystery of the Rosary.

- One minute reflections on each mystery to guide you on the go.

- In-depth reflections to draw you into contemplation with each mystery of the Rosary.

Paperback, 3.5"x5.5", 92 pages

$4.00

Available at LifeTeen.com/Store

○ LIFE TEEN